·NEW YORK CITY GUIDE·

Ny & About

BY MARTHA SACHSER

2021

IF YOU CAN **DREAM IT,**
YOU CAN **DO IT.**

WALT DISNEY

To my father, **Hilbert**,
for believing in me
even when I didn't
believe in myself.
And to my mother, **Dina**,
for not letting me give up
not even in my wildest dreams.
My eternal gratitude for the life they
gave me and for
the dreams, they have
allowed me to live.

HELLO
New York

Nice to meet you, my name is **Martha Sachser**. I am a photographer of the world's most incredible clients, author of the blog **NY & About** and passionate about everything New York, the city where I have been living since 2010.

After receiving many requests from followers, I decided to create a N.Y.C. guide with an itinerary that has everything to do with me:

Here you'll find history, music, must-see attractions, shopping and lots of good food!

My goal is to share everything that makes me happy here in a simple and organized way, so you can enjoy your days in New York as much as possible and save yourself time and money!

But don't get caught up in the guide; feel free to find your favorite restaurants and hidden gems around the city, let New York surprise you. Also, check out the many other cool tips on the **blog** whenever you need more new ideas!

Don't forget to share your favorite adventures with me on social media, I would love to hear from you!

Lastly, just pack your suitcase and get ready for the incredible days that await you, your itinerary is ready!

I Love New York!
And I'm one of those who believe that love is even better when it's shared!

HAVE FUN, AND SEE YOU NEXT TIME!

XOXO,

Martha

INDEX

DAY BY DAY

This guide was written in a practical way, so you can enjoy your trip wholeheartedly and return home with a feeling of having experienced both: the more touristy New York and some of New Yorkers' favorite places!

Here is what the itinerary looks like, so you can condense one day's activities with another and pick up the pace and customize as you wish. Keep in mind that days like Thursday, Friday and Saturday are planned to end the day at fun places.

Have a nice trip!

SUNDAY (DAY 01)

5th Avenue | Grand Central Terminal | United Nations | Bryant Park | Herald Square | Koreatown | Times Square

MONDAY (DAY 02)

Upper East Side | MET | Central Park | Roosevelt Tram

TUESDAY (DAY 03)

Upper West Side | Broadway Show

WEDNESDAY (DAY 04)

Flatiron | Madison Square Park | SoHo | Chinatown | Little Italy | Union Square

THURSDAY (DAY 05)

Statue of Liberty | Financial District | Downtown | East Village

FRIDAY (DAY 06)

West Village | Chelsea | High Line Park | Meatpacking District

SATURDAY (DAY 07)

Brooklyn Bridge | DUMBO | Williamsburg

SUNDAY (DAY 08)

Harlem

MONDAY (DAY 09)

Long Island City | Astoria

TUESDAY (DAY 10)

Hoboken | New Jersey | Outlets

WEDNESDAY (DAY 11)

The Bronx

THURSDAY (DAY 12)

Brooklyn Prospect Park | Botanical Garden

FRIDAY (DAY 13)

Coney Island

SATURDAY (DAY 14)

Corona | Flushing

SUNDAY (DAY 15)

Governors Island | Red Hook

MONDAY (DAY 16)

Rockaway Beach (Summer)

THE ITINERARY

This itinerary was created based on the days of the week. For example, days like Thursday, Friday and Saturday are inclined to be more exciting and good for nightlife. Not every street or nice bar will be fun on a Monday night. If you don't take this into consideration, feel free to move things around, of course. Things are always happening in New York so, do what you want while you are here.

It's very common for businesses to close here and there and the attractions hours of operations may change, so if you are going somewhere out of your route or don't wanna get frustrated, google the place to make sure the information is still valid.

The first week was dedicated to places that I believe are the must-see places on your first trip. The second week covers all the "not so obvious" locations and neighborhoods, perfect for anyone who wants to explore New York even more and feel even more like a local.

Most streets and avenues are numbered, but not every neighborhood is like that, it is common to get confused. Don't be ashamed to ask around for help, New Yorkers are used to it and, if they aren't in a rush, they love to help.

The book mentions the price for many attractions but keep in mind that the majority of them are included in attraction passes such as CityPASS, The Sightseeing Pass, etc. Prices also might change every year, so make sure to check the official websites before you go.

FREQUENTLY ASKED QUESTIONS ABOUT NEW YORK

1 Immigration at NYC's airports

It might be a little intimidating for some people, but if you have everything that is required to enter the US (visa, enough money - cash or card – proof of accommodation and return ticket), you have nothing to worry about. The chance of something going wrong is very small. Immigration officials usually ask basic questions like: How many days are you going to stay in the city/What is the purpose of your trip?/How much money have you brought?...If you don't speak English don't worry, they know that you are a foreigner and if you have a hard time understanding the immgration officer, simply ask for a translator. But seriously, you should be fine, just print out all the information before your trip.

2 How Much Does It Cost To Travel To New York?

It might sound cliché, but the final price literally depends on your priority, the time of year and the number of people who you'll share the cost of the accommodation with - because it is the most expensive part, in addition to airfare. But I will try to break down the prices here and throughout the book.

Accomodation

An average rate for a simple/good hotel in Manhattan ranges from $150-300. There are options to reduce this cost, such as staying at hotels in some parts of Brooklyn and Queens - especially Long Island City, which is very close to Manhattan. The average daily rate is around $120 - $200.
Staying at a hostel can be a good alternative to save money and to make friends. Prices range from $35-$80 per person. To search and book accommodation in hostels I suggest checking hostels.com.

You can also save money by staying at an *Airbnb*. **Oh!** And reading reviews is crucial when choosing the right one, it can be risky if you don't have good recommendations.

Transportation

Subway or taxi? Subway in NY is quite cheap, fast, efficient, operates 24 hours a day and takes you everywhere. So, I strongly recommend using it! It may seem complicated and intimidating at first, but with practice, GPS and a subway map in hand, you'll be a pro In only a few days!

Food

How much does food cost in NY? Is it possible to eat healthy? Yes! And it depends on what you like, but don't worry, you can find all kinds of food and prices here! From $1 pizza slices to the most sophisticated restaurants! From organic to fast-food! Needless to say, pretty much every corner you look, you will find a pharmacy or a deli that sells snacks which you can bring with you for a quick bite between meals.

If you have a refrigerator at your hotel, you can also stop by a supermarket and buy some things to prepare sandwiches, etc.

FREQUENTLY

ASKED
QUESTIONS
ABOUT
**NEW
YORK**

3   Which locations are the best to stay?

This is also very relative. Even though many people dream of being in the heart of Times Square, I believe this shouldn't restrain your search. Manhattan has attractions and points of interest all over and each neighborhood has an unique character. But overall, I always suggest staying close to a subway station, as the system operates 24 hours a day and reaches pretty much every neighborhood in the whole city. But my favorite areas are West Village, SoHo, Upper West Side, Midtown and Williamsburg.

4   Which Broadway Show to Watch?
Is It Worth the Investment?

The prices vary by the show, but an average cost would be $32-$90 per person for standard mezzanine/balcony or sale tickets. Recommending **one** musical is difficult since there are several must-sees! Knowing whether the investment is worth it or not depends on the type of entertainment you prefer, so my advice is: find out what musicals are playing and check out the ones that are more to your taste! Also, **consider your level of English**! For those with beginner level, I wouldn't recommend a show like the *Book of Mormons* for instance. If you don't have anything specific in mind you can't go wrong with *The Phantom of the Opera*, *Aladdin*, *Hamilton*, *Wicked* or *The Lion King*.

5   Is There Wi-Fi Everywhere or
should I get a sim card?

There is public wi-fi in countless corners around the city, in some parks, subway stations, McDonald's, Starbucks, restaurants and many shops. But depending on your need to use the internet, as well to save time and simplify your mobility, it might be worth investing in a sim card. When you arrive in New York, I recommend going to a T-Mobile or AT&T store. They'll offer you different plans but with $40-$50 you can get decent coverage.

6   Is it possible to travel to NY and not speak any English?

Generally yes, and many people travel here under those circumstances. The entire world is here, most likely you will find someone who speaks your language at random places and maybe it will work out! In New York, a lot of people also speak Spanish in stores, restaurants, and hotels. If you don't speak English at all, plan your trip properly before traveling (picking places to visit, find out how much things cost …). Having internet access also makes it much easier (so you can use translators, look for directions, make reservations, etc).

7 What is the weather like during each season?

❄ November | December

In November, the average temperature is 5-12°C/ 41-54°F but you might experience lower temperatures as well or maybe you are lucky and warmer days will welcome you. By the second half of December, the temperature drops a bit more and it's common to get around 0-8° C / 32- 46°F) or sometimes lower. It doesn't snow as often as many people think during this period, it's most likely to snow between January - February but it's New York, so you never know. The sun sets around 4:30 pm and it is usually very windy.

☃ January | February | March

In these 3 months of winter it usually gets remarkably cold, between -5° C and 5° C (between 23°F and 41°F) and it is very difficult to stay outdoors for long periods due to the wind. The chances of snow are much higher and the cold is persistent. It doesn't snow as much as people think in general and we usually get at least one or two snow storms. Generally schools are cancelled that day and the following. Some businesses remain open and flights may get canceled.

❀ April | May

It slowly begins to feel more like spring towards the second half of April. Average temperature ranges from 7-16°C/ 45-61°F. In the beginning of May you can expect the temperature to be between 12-22°C / 54- 72°F during the day, but it gets even warmer by the end of the month. The weather is hard to predict during spring and fall. But typically, May offers wonderful days to enjoy the city, which gets beautiful with flowers all over!

☀ June | July | August

June is when the heat strikes, but it gets even more intense in July and August. During these months, the temperature can reach 40°C (104°F) with high humidity... it feels like a sauna! Although in the last 2 years, I found summer to be cooler, except for subway stations, they are still hot as an oven. But there are many events and activities, so it makes it all worth it. The sun sets around 8:30pm during the summer, plenty of time to enjoy the city!!

🌳 September | October

My favorite months! From the second half of September the temperature gets cooler (16-24°C / 61-75°F), perfect for enjoying all the best that NY has to offer without heat waves. In October, autumn begins and in the first two weeks the weather is usually nice (10-18°C / 50-64°F). In the second half of the month, temperatures drop a bit more (6-17°C / 43-63°F). It doesn't get unbearable in my opinion, but often there are a few colder and windy days. It is beautiful to see Central Park when the trees' leaves change color, they usually reach their peak between October 25 and the first week of November. The days begin to get dark around 6 pm.

8 Is New York a dangerous city?

I don't believe there is a place on earth that is 100% safe. You can find people with bad intentions everywhere. But yes, I think NYC in general is really safe and in the past 10 years of living here, I have never had any issues with personal safety. The feeling of safety is very strong, you can go around carrying your cell phone, computer, tablet, and camera almost everywhere. However you may see people with mental disorders, homeless and beggars especially on the subway. Just pay attention to your surroundings and be smart, but they are usually harmless.

9 Do I have to tip?

YES! In general you are expected to tip 15%-25% of the total amount of the bill. Some services aren't paid according to percentages, e.g.: people who help you with your bags, a hotel concierge who helps you with a taxi, etc. For some services tips aren't expected but are appreciated. Here are a few suggestions:

Taxi
Between 15% and 20%

Waiter
Between 18% and 25%
Large groups may automatically have a tip included in the bill.

Bartender
$1 per drink minimum at the bar or more if the drink is expensive

Bar and restaurants' coat check
$1 to $5

Self-service restaurants' cashiers
Tips are not required, but they are appreciated.

Hotel Housekeeping
I suggest a minimum of $2 per day

Bellhops
U$1-2 per bag

Things to know: Many workers need tips to survive because they don't make minimum wage from their company, so even if you disagree with this practice, you are still expected to pay it here in the United States.

HOW TO USE THE SUBWAY

The subway system is the way to go when exploring NYC. Here are some important information to make your experience even better:

The trains run 24 hours, although a little less frequently late at night. Some lines with similar routes may merge and some express trains may run local (like the E train for example). But overall at least from early morning to late at night, you should be okay using the subway.

◆ Track maintenance and subway station renovations are very frequent and usually take place in the middle of the night and on weekends or sometimes during the day when it isn't so busy, before rush hour. To avoid unpleasant surprises I recommend downloading the MYmta app, or pay attention to paper announcements at stations for track changes. You can also check the official mta website (new.mta.info) for the updated weekend map and any other notification about every line.

◆ The subway fare is U$2.75 per trip. The metrocard costs US$1. Keep your card to reload if necessary, that way you don't need to buy another card. You can share the same card with 3 other people at a time if you get a regular card, but you can't share if you buy an unlimited ride card.

◆ Make sure to download the *NYC Subway Map*, *Citymapper* and *Google Maps* (or any other navigator) to get around the city by subway.

◆ The subway covers all boroughs in NYC! There are over 470 stations and 27 lines (in 2020). It sounds like a lot, but it's only to show you that you will probably be able to go anywhere by subway and if you happen to miss a stop or get lost, it's okay, you can always turn around and take the train in the opposite direction or get off at the station and walk if you are close to your destination.

◆ The subway stations might be a little intimidating at first, but the signs and directions are usually straightforward. If you are confused, ask for help.

◆ Familiarize yourself with the subway map before your visit. The official subway map is also the map of the city, you can clearly see where each borough is located and you can understand the directions you will be using when visiting, such as: Queens, Brooklyn, Bronx, Manhattan, Uptown, Upper East Side, Upper West Side, Lower East Side, Downtown, East Side and so on. Geographic coordinates are important to understand NYC. Most streets and Avenues in Manhattan are numbered. The Village and the older part (Downtown) is much more complicated, but with a GPS and a map in hand you should be fine!

◆ So, let's say you are at Grand Central Terminal (which is located on 42nd Street) and you want to go to The Metropolitan Museum of Art (which is located between 80th and 84th Streets). You saw on the map that the trains 4,5,6, stop near the museum. So which direction would you take the subway? Uptown? Downtown? Well, Uptown would be the right answer, since you are on 42nd Street and need to go "up" to 80th street. See? It isn't hard, just learn your East and West and you will be good to go. Or simply rely on technology, Google maps is good enough to get around and you will be fine.

◆ You will see some lines running on the same tracks at times, but it doesn't mean they have the same final destination. Open the subway map and find lines 4, 5 and 6. Now notice how they are running basically on the same tracks in Manhattan, but they are running on different routes in the Bronx and Brooklyn.

◆ There are local trains, which means they will stop at all stations on that line. And there are the express trains, those skip many stations and stop at the main and usually busiest ones where the local trains also stop. So make sure you are taking the right train by reading the signs and checking your subway map: the stops with a black dot on the map mean that the train is local and the stops with a white dot means they are express trains.

◆ There are often beggars and homeless on the trains. They are usually harmless and most likely sooner or later, you will see people performing on the trains as well, they expect a tip, or sometimes a smile. If you film or take photos they expect a tip.

◆ NYC subway is by no means the cleanest or most modern, but it is quite efficient. If you need help, look for an MTA booth or use the Help Point on platforms for emergencies. MTA stands for Metropolitan Transportation Authority. It is the largest public transportation agency in North America and one of the largest in the world. There are millions of people using public transportation in NYC every day.

1 BUS STATION
BUS AND TRAINS WITH DIFFERENT DESTINATIONS

Port Authority Bus Terminal | *www.panynj.gov/bus-terminals*
New Jersey Transit | *www.njtransit.com*
Long Island Rail Road | *lirr42.mta.info*
Amtrak | *www.amtrak.com*

2 INTERCITY BUSES - TRAVELING ON A BUDGET

Some private companies offer tickets to other nice cities for reasonable prices! Some destinations on the list include Washington DC, Baltimore, Philadelphia, Boston and Atlantic City. The buses are not super comfortable, but the experience of traveling around on a budget is worth it.

www.boltbus.com
www.megabus.com
www.gotobus.com
www.flixbus.com
www.greyhound.com
www.peterpanbus.com
www.wanderu.com

3 SITES TO BOOK HOTELS, HOSTELS, CAR RENTAL
OR BUY AIRLINE TICKETS

Renting cars here is very simple. Most companies accept a driver's license from different countries and you only need to have a credit card (that works here).

www.kayak.com
www.expedia.com
www.priceline.com
www.hotwire.com
www.booking.com
www.hostels.com
www.hotels.com

Besides hostels and AirBnB there are some hotels that offer competitive prices. Many of my readers have shared their favorites with me when traveling on a (not so tight) budget to NY:

In Manhattan

Yotel
POD Times Square
The Row
Paramount
Citizen M
Wellington Hotel
Hotel St. James
Edison Hotel
Belnord
The Watson Hotel
DoubleTree by Hilton
POD 51
La Quinta Inn (near Central Park)
Park Central
Hilton Garden Inn
Residence Inn by Marriott
Novotel Times Square
Night Hotel Times Square
Belvedere Hotel
Hotel 31

In Queens

Queens County Inn and Suites
Aloft
Royal Stay
Red Lion Inn & Suites
Quality Inn Long Island City
Fairfield Inn& Suites by Marriott
Holiday Inn

HOSTELS
in New York

If you love traveling and saving money as I do, you are probably already familiar with the word "hostel". If you are a solo traveler or traveling on a budget, check out some of the favorite hostels my followers stayed and recommended in NYC:

HI NEW YORK HOSTELLING INTERNATIONAL
891 Amsterdam Avenue
Hostelling International hostels usually have nice quality standards for services such as comfort and cleaning, which are very important. The hostel is situated away from the midtown buzz, located in a much quieter area, on the Upper West Side. Room options vary from shared to private or with or without bathrooms. Furthermore, the hostel is filled with activities, tours, and events for travelers. Some special rooms have breakfast included, but the hostel also has a small restaurant where you can buy your meals and a fully equipped kitchen, so you can prepare whatever you like.

JAZZ ON COLUMBUS CIRCLE
940 8th Avenue
Located in one of the most central areas of Manhattan, Jazz on Columbus Circle is one of my favorites in New York! Besides the location, which is close to Times Square, Central Park, Columbus Circle and Lincoln Center, you can find several restaurants close by, clean accommodation and they also offer shared, private or family rooms.

AMERICAN DREAM HOSTEL

168 East 24th Street, between Lexington and 3rd Ave
www.americandreamhostel.com

For those who want some privacy, this is a good spot. Located at the charming and quiet area of Gramercy Park and Flatiron District and with access to restaurants, bars, and Union Square, the rooms at American Hostel are private with one, two or three beds and equipped with TV, air conditioning, and even a sink! Bathrooms are shared, but located on the same floor. Another plus: Breakfast is included and there is free wi-fi! The cost is a bit higher than other hostels and the atmosphere is close to a bed and breakfast style. The rate per person in 2020 started at $79 per night. Fees not included.

WILLIAMSBURG MOORE HOSTEL

179 Moore Street | www.nymoorehostel.com

Located in Williamsburg, but with easy access to Manhattan, this is for those who want to feel the atmosphere outside Manhattan in one of the youngest and most groovy areas of the city. You'll find plenty of bars, restaurants, galleries ... The hostel has a cool vibe, with art on the walls plus a common area to relax and meet other travelers! It doesn't include breakfast, but there is a fully equipped kitchen, so you can prepare meals and they also have tea and coffee available all day long. They also offer events like movie night, comedy shows, and others.

THE LOCAL NYC

1302 44th Ave | thelocalny.com

Located in Long Island City, Queens, The Local NYC has long been one of the travelers' favorite hostels. Besides the modern vibe, being clean and organized, there is a bar and a terrace overlooking the city. Despite the fact that it is off the Manhattan island it is possible to reach midtown within minutes by subway and by ferry. The hostel offers coin washing machines and dryers and a fully equipped kitchen. Although they don't serve breakfast, you can buy it at the bar in the hostel! Long Island City Is experiencing a boom and opening more spots for housing and, although it looks quieter compared to Manhattan, it is very safe.

OTHER GREAT HOSTELS AND HOTELS WORTH CHECKING OUT IN NY:
YMCA HOSTELS |BROADWAY HOSTEL | CHELSEA INTERNATIONAL HOSTEL |
THE JANE | CENTRAL PARK WEST HOSTEL

What to do in the winter in Nyc?

One of the most frequently asked questions is about the weather in NY during winter months and if it is as cruel as people say. And well, yes, there are nice days, but there are really cold days as well. Does that mean the city stops and you can't do anything? No. Everything works just the same, however, it takes a little more planning to get the most out of the city, like considering the time of day when it starts to get darker (around 4:30 pm). So, I picked some attractions and cool activities to do in the winter on regular days and on extremely cold days.

PHOTO SHOOTS

Some of my favorite travel memories come from photo shoots and winter in New York is beyond charming, so it deserves to be remembered in beautiful photographs. To book your photo session contact me through my website (*marthasachserphotography.com*) and mention you have my book for a special discount!

ICE SKATING

This is one of my favorite winter traditions! Starting at the end of October, with the temperature dropping and winter coming up, ice skating is a great activity for the whole family. My favorite rink is the Wollman, in Central Park. The prices range for different rinks, among the top 3 most famous, the most expensive is the Rink At Rockefeller Center and the cheapest is the one in Bryant Park. But there are other rinks available, check the blog (www.nyandabout.com/en) for prices and details!

VISIT NEW YORK'S TRAIN STATIONS

Penn Station and Grand Central Terminal are the city's most famous and busiest train stations. There, you will not only find thousands of people rushing around trying to catch their trains but you can also find unique restaurants, snack bars and shops. Grand Central Terminal is my favorite and it is gorgeous, but for those who want to take a bite of local life, I recommend visiting them both if you have the chance!

GO BOWLING WHILE LISTENING TO LIVE MUSIC!

61 Wythe Avenue, Brooklyn | www.brooklynbowl.com
The Brooklyn Bowl goes beyond just conventional bowling, besides playing and getting something to eat you will enjoy live bands and delicious drinks!

EXPLORE THE (MANY) MUSEUMS

Despite being one of the most sought-after destinations on rainy, cold days, you still should have in mind that there are a bazillion museums in New York. Many of them are free, others paid and some pay as you want. Try the not so obvious ones to avoid crowded museums.

HAVE FUN AT DAVE AND BUSTERS

234 W 42nd Street, New York
Cold days can become fun ones, especially if you are traveling with kids! At Dave and Busters, you will find many arcade games for the whole family! As you play you collect tickets that you can exchange for toys and more at the end of the night. It's pretty cool and the kids (and adults) will love it for sure. Plus, it has a restaurant that serves typical American food: lots of burgers, salads, pasta and of course, french fries!

EXPLORE THE CITY'S BOOK STORES

One thing that really brings me joy is knowing that despite the amount of technology we have, New York still has a large variety of beautiful bookstores for us to dive into and experience without ever leaving the room. Not to mention the super cozy cafes that sometimes come with them.

Barnes and Noble *(33 E 17th Street)*: This bookstore chain has its megastore at Union Square, however you can also find other stores around the city. In addition to books, they also have office and home decor, board games and toys, eBook readers and of course, a coffee shop. A big number of events take place over there as well as readings and Q and A's where you can meet the author and get a signed copy of the book!

Shakespeare and Co *(939 Lexington Avenue)*: Charming and not as crowded as the others. Besides books, It also has a small café and is located in a less touristy part of the city.

Housing Works Bookstore Cafe & Bar *(130 Crosby Street)*: This is a beautiful used books bookstore with a nice cafe in the back. Everything is very clean and in good condition, worth checking out! Next to it you will find a Housing Works thrift shop.

McNally Jackson *(52 Prince Street)*: You will be sure to find me there any day of the year but it is the perfect destination when walking around the streets of SoHo. There are other branches, but this is my favorite. There is also a cafe inside.

Strand Book Store *(828 Broadway)*: Over 18 miles of books are waiting for you at this iconic bookstore near Union Square! They offer new and used titles, souvenirs and stationery.

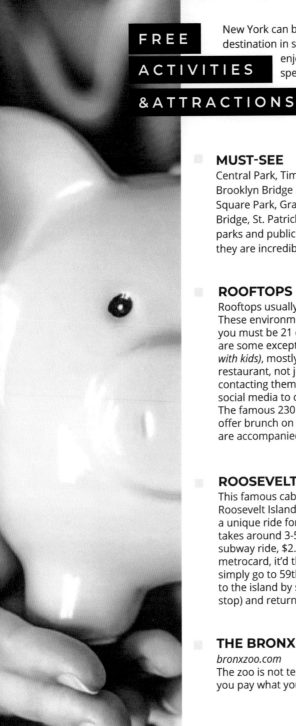

FREE ACTIVITIES & ATTRACTIONS

New York can be considered an expensive destination in some ways, but overall you can enjoy most of the city without spending a dime or as much money as you might expect. Here are some of my favorites:

MUST-SEE

Central Park, Times Square, High Line Park, Brooklyn Bridge Park, 9/11 Memorial, Washington Square Park, Grand Central Terminal, Brooklyn Bridge, St. Patrick's Cathedral and many other parks and public areas are completely free and they are incredible!

ROOFTOPS

Rooftops usually don't charge entrance fees. These environments serve alcoholic beverages, you must be 21 or over to get in, although there are some exceptions *(check page 64 if traveling with kids)*, mostly when the rooftop is also a restaurant, not just a bar. In these cases, I suggest contacting them directly via e-mail/phone or social media to confirm if they allow kids to enter. The famous 230 5th Avenue is one of those that offer brunch on weekends and admit minors that are accompanied during brunch hours.

ROOSEVELT ISLAND TRAM

This famous cable car connecting Manhattan to Roosevelt Island offers a fabulous view and is a unique ride for the whole family! The journey takes around 3-5 minutes and costs only a subway ride, $2.75. If you get the unlimited metrocard, it'd theoretically be free! To get there simply go to 59th Street and 1st Avenue or get to the island by subway (Line F- Roosevelt Island stop) and return to Manhattan by tram.

THE BRONX ZOO

bronxzoo.com
The zoo is not technically free but on Wednesdays you pay what you want.

FREE WALKING TOUR

freetoursbyfoot.com/new-york-tours
One of the coolest things created in this travel world is the free walking tour. I had a great experience in the past and I definitely recommend it. How it works: The tour is free, however at the end, if you enjoyed it, you should tip your guide. People usually tip them between $5 and $20. You should be reasonable and pay what you think is fair or what your budget allows, but a suggestion is at least $5 if it is a very large group. There are several tours to various parts of the city.

STATEN ISLAND FERRY

If you don't want to spend money to see the Statue of Liberty up close, you can take the free ferry that connects Manhattan to Staten Island with a beautiful view of downtown! And the best part? It costs nothing! The ride takes about 25 minutes and the ferry leaves every 20-30 minutes normally or every 15 minutes during rush hour. How do you get to the ferry terminal? You can take the subway, the closest are 1 (South Ferry station), R, W (Whitehall Street station) 4 or 5 (Bowling Green station), J or Z (Broad Street station). Look for the Staten Island Ferry Terminal.

MUSEUMS

There are many, many, many museums in New York. Some are free, most are paid and some have a suggested price, in which you can pay any amount as you like. But the good news is usually once a week, on a specific day and time, there will be no entry fee. MoMa, for example, doesn't charge on Fridays between 4-8pm. I listed some of my favorite museums throughout the book!

THE VESSEL

www.hudsonyardsnewyork.com/reserve
The biggest private real estate development in the U.S., Hudson Yards is the new must-see in NYC and it brings with it the Vessel, this sculpture with 2500 steps that lead to nowhere – there is also an elevator. This unique design was created by Thomas Heatherwick. You can get tickets for free on the official website or you can try same day tickets using one of the kiosks or in person heading up to the 4th floor inside the Beyond the Edge store.

FREE ADMISSION ATTRACTIONS

Another thing to have in mind, not only museums, but places like Botanical gardens, aquariums, zoos and so on, most likely will have free admission or a pay what you wish policy on specific days and hours. Unfortunately some places have changed their policies during the COVID-19 pandemic so make sure you check before you visit. The Brooklyn Botanical Garden for example is currently offering Community Tickets, for those who can't afford the entrance fee.

MOVIE NIGHTS

www.nycgovparks.org/events/free_summer_movies
If you are visiting New York in the summer months, most likely you will be able to catch a movie under the stars at some of the most famous NYC parks, such as Brooklyn Bridge Park, Bryant Park and Central Park. Grab a snack, a blanket and watch a movie for free! You can check the park's social media and website for details.

FREE CONCERTS!

There are countless free concerts happening throughout the city, but there are two that everyone talks about: the NBC's Today Concert Series and ABC's Good Morning America Summer Series. Also, the Summerstage Festival in Central Park is a popular one! Check their official websites for schedules and more info!

ENJOY THE DAY ON GOVERNORS ISLAND

govisland.com
From May to October Governors Island is the perfect place to escape the city without having to cross any bridges! Once a military base, the island is now the most popular "playground" for New Yorkers! Check *page 60* for more about it. But even though the ferry ride costs $3 roundtrip, it's free before 11:30am on weekends! You can take the ferry at the Battery Maritime Building, right by the Staten Island ferry station! Check the official website for the schedule and other important information!

FREE KAYAKING

Yes, you read it right, there is free kayaking available throughout the city! You can rent yours at Downtown Boathouse at Pier 26 at Hudson River Park (*www.downtownboathouse.org*) and Manhattan Community Boathouse (*www. manhattancommunityboathouse.org*). It's such a unique experience! There are also locations in Long Island City (*www.licboathouse.org*) and Brooklyn (*www.bbpboathouse.org*)

METROPOLITAN OPERA

www.metopera.org
If you are a big fan of Opera this is a must. Of course, you can always buy a ticket and go see it live inside, but in the summer months, Lincoln Center offers an experience under the stars to watch the streaming outside the opera shows.

SHAKESPEARE IN THE PARK

www.publictheater.org/en/Programs--Events/Shakespeare-in-the-Park/
This is another favorite during the summer months. You can get your free tickets at the Delacorte Theater in Central Park from 12pm, when they start the distribution. Try to get there earlier. You can get 2 tickets per person. You can also try the Today Tix lottery or try the standby line later.

NEW YORK PHILHARMONIC

www.centralparknyc.org/things-to-see-and-do/new-york-philharmonic-concert.html
If you are in the city, make sure to grab a blanket, some snacks and drinks and head to Central Park on the night of the world famous New York Philharmonic Concert.

CONEY ISLAND & FIREWORKS SHOW

In addition to the beach and the boardwalk with many restaurants and shops, in the summer months on Friday nights, you can catch their traditional fireworks show on the beach! More on Coney Island later in the book!

BREAKFAST
in New York

Another thing that shocks many people who visit NY for the first time is finding out that most hotels don't offer breakfast. Yes, despite the considerably high rates, a few of them have this amenity and others charge separately to provide a breakfast buffet. So, I'll suggest some breakfast places that I think are nice to check out, but you will see options all over the book and I'm sure you will find nice options exploring the city on your own.

 ## BAGELS, BAGELS, BAGELS

If there is one thing that is part of most New Yorker's breakfast (and often lunch), it is a bagel, a type of bread that originated in the Jewish communities of Eastern Europe! You will lose count of how many bagel shops you will pass by in NY and you can choose from what seems to be endless fillings and cream cheese flavors! Traditional bagels cost an average of $2 to $5. When in doubt of what to order, go for everything OR plain bagel toasted with cream cheese! You can't go wrong!

Some bagel shops I love:
Ess-a-Bagel | *www.ess-a-bagel.com*
Murray's Bagels | *www.murraysbagels.com*
H&H Midtown Bagels | *hhmidtownbagels.com/store/pc/viewCategories.asp*
Sadelle's | *www.sadelles.com*
The Bagel Store | *www.thebagelstoreonline.com*
Black Seed Bagels | *www.blackseedbagels.com*
Russ & Daughters | *www.russanddaughters.com*
Kossar's | *kossars.com*
Best Bagel and Coffee | *www.bestbagelandcoffee.com*

 ## CHAIN RESTAURANTS AND COFFEE SHOPS

Coffee shops are all over the city and go beyond Starbucks and Dunkin Donuts. But if you don't have too much time to choose the perfect one, here are some famous coffee chains in NYC: Blue Bottle, Gregorys Coffee, Joe & The Juice, Irving Farm New York, Pret-a-Manger, La Colombe, Think Coffee, Paris Baguette and Le Pain Quotidien. For those on a budget try Dunkin Donuts, McDonald's, 7-Eleven and coffee carts, especially in midtown and delis in general (a market that sells food to go - some have seating available) where you can get yourself a cup of coffee and something simple for less than U$5.

IHOP

A classic American style breakfast, iHop (*235 East 14th Street | www.ihop.com/ en/menu*) is famous for serving pancakes, omelets, waffles... The menu and the portions are generous and the prices are reasonable.

ELLEN'S STARDUST

This iconic and fun diner in New York usually has long queues at lunch and dinner time, but usually goes unnoticed at breakfast time! As you eat, the waiters perform and sing several hits! Overall, the food is okay (nothing incredible), but the whole experience is pretty cool! It is located at 1650 Broadway.

LADURÉE

The charming French chain offers, in addition to macarons, other delicacies such as assorted croissants, cakes, toast, and omelets plus drinks to start the day with energy. The largest store and my favorite is the one in SoHo. They have a set menu ($17 or $33) for breakfast in the morning, but you can also ask for other single items as well. Check updated prices and the menu here: *www.laduree.us | It is located at 398 West Broadway.*

STARBUCKS RESERVE NEW YORK ROASTERY

One of the few in the world, this Starbucks experience is for those who love coffee and perhaps never considered Starbucks. Yes, you will be amazed by the options available here, from coffee tasting to alcoholic coffee inspired drinks. And pastries, sandwiches and much more for that perfect breakfast! It is located at 61 9th Ave.

LITTLE CUPCAKE BAKESHOP

Cakes, cheesecakes, croissants, cookies, sweet tarts, coffees, teas... This cute little place in SoHo is busy all day long. They also offer vegan and gluten-free options, so it's worth the stop! It is located at 30 Prince Street. It opens at 7:30 am on weekdays and at 8am on weekends.

BROOKLYN DINER

A classic American style diner. It is an upscale diner, but It is very casual at the same time. The food is good but nothing outstanding in my opinion. Still, for those who want a different and quieter experience, this is a nice place. The Brooklyn Diner has two addresses in New York: 212 West 57th Street and 155 West 43rd Street.

EMERGENCY NUMBERS

Emergencies: *911*
Non- emergencies: *311 or 212-NEW-YORK (639-9675)*
JFK Lost and Found: *(718) 751-4001*
Subway Lost and Found: *511*
Newark Liberty International Airport: *(973) 961-6000*
John F. Kennedy International Airport: *(718) 244-4444*
LaGuardia Airport: *(718) 533-3400*
Stewart Airport: *(845) 838-8200*

20 PLACES TO VISIT ON YOUR FIRST TRIP TO NEW YORK

- Central Park
- Statue of Liberty
- Metropolitan Museum of Art, MoMa and/or Museum of Natural History
- Brooklyn Bridge
- High Line Park
- 9/11 Memorial
- Times Square
- West Village
- A fun rooftop bar
- Grand Central Terminal
- Top of the Rock, Empire State Building, Edge, One World Observatory or The Summit
- Little Italy
- Chinatown
- Brooklyn Bridge Park
- DUMBO
- Wall Street
- Stone Street
- Battery Park City
- Williamsburg
- SoHo

NYC IN MOVIES

If you are traveling to NYC, there are countless movies that will inspire you to explore more of the city, here are 25 of my favorites:

- Home Alone 2
- 13 Going on 30
- Enchanted
- Serendipity
- King Kong
- Miracle on 34th Street
- Friends With Benefits
- Breakfast at Tiffany's
- You've Got Mail
- Sex and The City
- BIG
- When Harry Met Sally
- Ghostbusters
- Elf
- The Devil Wears Prada
- Spider Man
- Men In Black
- Wolf of Wall Street
- The Godfather
- Made of honor
- No Reservations
- What Happens in Vegas
- Music and Lyrics
- Maid in Manhattan
- Ghost

BRUNCH IN NYC

Weekends mean brunch time in NYC! For those who don't know, brunch is that amazing breakfast enhanced with pancakes, waffles, sandwiches, eggs of all kinds and of course, mimosas and other traditional brunch drinks. Brunch gathers friends and family to this laid- back meal which is so New York! I've selected places that have already appeared on the blog and are worth checking out but you will see options all over the book.

BUBBY'S

120 Hudson Street | www.bubbys.com
Bubby's is a classic restaurant located in Tribeca. Here the pancakes are the stars of the brunch but you can get them for breakfast as well any day of the week.

ASIATE

80 Columbus Circle at 60th Street | www.mandarinoriental.com/new-york
For a more sophisticated and delicious experience, Asiate is a great pick! With breathtaking views of Central Park and Columbus Circle, the restaurant is inside the Mandarin Oriental Hotel. The restaurant is modern, upscale, and has an impressive selection of wines. For those who desire to start the day here with an American menu option, be sure to order the Smoked Salmon Eggs Benedict with English muffin, french toast or a Belgian waffle. Brunch costs $64 per person (plus tip, drinks, and fees) with appetizer, entrée, and dessert.

CLINTON STREET BAKING COMPANY

4 Clinton Street | www.clintonstreetbaking.com
Super tasty brunch option on weekends, portions are generous. Most dishes are between $12-18 and there is usually a long line on weekends. To avoid a long wait on weekends, they say you can arrive by 8:30 AM to get in line and be one of the first when they open at 9 AM. If not, once you put your name on the list, the wait can be as long as 1 or close to 2 hours. If you hate waiting they recommend on the website that you visit during the week or at night.

CORNER STONE CAFE

17 Avenue B | www.cornerstonecafenyc.com/brunch
This is a simple and cozy restaurant in the Lower East Side, one of the areas with a more local vibe and that is worth the visit (I've got you, it's in the itinerary). Nice atmosphere and portions at a fair price (most dishes cost less than $15) but we had to wait a bit to sit down, so plan ahead and if your stomach starts growling and the line is too long, Avenue B is surrounded by super cool restaurants for a traditional brunch too!

 ## THE RABBIT HOLE

352 Bedford Ave (Between 3rd Street and 4th Street) | www.rabbitholerestaurant.com
Located in Williamsburg, Brooklyn, the restaurant's simple and rustic decor has earned my heart since the first time I went there and I could not leave it off this list! The average cost per dish is $10-15. Cocktail prices are around $11.

 ## CECCONI'S AND CELESTINE

Sitting between Brooklyn and Manhattan Bridge, Cecconi's offers beautiful views of the East River and is located in DUMBO, one of my favorite places in NY. The brunch menu includes some of the classics and most main dishes cost between $12-20. It is located at 55 Water Street.

Another restaurant close by is Celestine, serving Eastern Meditarranean food by the Manhattan Bridge. The main dishes are between $15-20 and they also have appetizers ($5-12). It is located at 1 John Street, Brooklyn.

PEACEFOOD CAFE

www.peacefoodcafe.com/menu/
One of my favorite vegan restaurants, Peacefood Cafe has more than one location, but my favorite location is in downtown: *41 East 11th Street.* Peacefood serves brunch on weekends and I'm always there. They have a nice selection of cakes, sandwiches, soups, waffles, smoothies, cheesecakes, brownies …I love it!

 TAVERN ON THE GREEN

www.tavernonthegreen.com/menu/brunch/
A New York classic, Tavern on the Green is in Central Park and is worth the experience itself! I've been there a few times on special occasions and I find the food good, nothing exceptional, but the overall experience is great…Take the rest of the day to enjoy the park if you can! The main dishes for brunch cost an average $26 and appetizers range $10-20. If you want to save some money, I advise going on another day of the week, when the menu is open and it offers more options.

 BRUNCH ON A MINI-CRUISE AROUND MANHATTAN
www.cityexperiences.com/new-york
Have you ever thought of having brunch cruising on the river overlooking Manhattan!? There are several companies that offer it, but I recommend checking City Experiences by Hornblower.

 230 FIFTH AVENUE
230 5ht Avenue | www.230-fifth.com
For those who are traveling with the family and want to experience a rooftop, this is a good alternative, guests under 21 can enter if accompanied by an adult! The bar offers brunch from 11 in the morning until 4 in the afternoon. The food is standard but overall It is a good experience. You don't need a reservation. However, if you are in a group larger than six people, contact them for booking!

New York has more vegan restaurants than I can count, so before you come, download the app *Happy Cow* to find more vegan restaurants near you. But here are some of my favorites:

CHAMPS DINER

197 Meserole St | www.champsdiner.com
This Brooklyn heaven serves a number of options that you could find in a standard American diner, from mac and cheese to the most delicious milkshakes, pancakes, and many sandwiches.

URBAN VEGAN KITCHEN

41 Carmine Street
www.urbanvegankitchen.com
Love their famous *Mac and Cheese*! Plus it serves a great brunch on weekends too. On commemorative dates, such as on Valentine's Day or Thanksgiving, there is always a fixed price menu for those who want to make a reservation! The atmosphere is cool with music playing in the background.

VSPOT

12 St. Marks Place
I love Latin food and I always eat at V Spot. The menu includes all the classics, from burritos and quesadillas to fried avocado and good drinks! The restaurant is on St. Marks Place, one of New York's funkiest streets. The prices are pretty okay, and you could have a good meal for less than $20. The restaurant is also part of the NYC Vegan Food Court, which means it shares the location with other vegan vendors/chefs.

VEGAN RESTAURANTS

RED BAMBOO

140 West 4th Street | www.redbamboo-nyc.com
With an extensive menu, you will find everything from wings and Philly cheesesteaks to teriyaki "chicken", pasta and "chicken" parmesan! They aren't 100% vegan, some dishes can be made with dairy, simply ask for vegan cheese to make sure it is 100% vegan! From appetizers to desserts, the portions are quite generous and not disappointing. Price is fine, many options under $15.

DUN WELL DOUGHNUTS

222 Montrose Avenue, Brooklyn | www.dunwelldoughnuts.com
Mojito, pineapple, pistachio, banana with peanut butter, lemon with coconut ...! These are some of Dun Well Donuts' super original and delicious flavors. Prices are also alright, each donut costs between $2.50 and $2.75. They accept cards however, there is a minimum of $10.

VAN LEEUWEN ICE CREAM

It's not entirely vegan, but offers a large variety of dairy-free options, from cookies and cream to strawberry cheesecake! From traditional tastes to the most unique ones! It has several locations in town but my favorite one is in the East Village, not far from some of the places mentioned above, such as VSpot.

SCREAMERS PIZZERIA

620 Manhattan Ave | www.screamerspizzeria.com
Screamer's Pizzeria is a must-go in Brooklyn! Cheese, Margherita, pepperoni, BBQ and many other amazing toppings! The pizzas are sold in slices or whole pie. Oh! Next to Screamers, there is also a Van Leeuwen!

RIVERDEL CHEESE

88 Essex Street | www.riverdelcheese.com
Cheese, cheese and more cheese! At Riverdel you can find a variety of other products, it is like a mini vegan market. But the big star is the cheese! I recommend the traditional cheese sandwich ($9) and the Italian ($10). Riverdel Cheese is located inside Essex Market in the Lower East Side.

FRANCHIA VEGAN CAFE

12 Park Ave (between 34th and 35th Streets) | www.franchia.com
The best of Asian cuisine, I find their dishes to be full of flavor and with wonderful presentation. It is always difficult to choose what to order, there are so many options! The ambiance is super nice, peaceful and zen and perfect for a dinner with friends or even a date with someone special. They also have many gluten-free options, awesome drinks, teas, tapas, vegan sushi plus a dessert menu!

PEACEFOOD CAFE

41 east 11th | www.peacefoodcafe.com/menu
From cookies to soups, everything is vegan and delicious! I recommend the pan seared shanghai-style dumplings (my favorite!), the unchicken basket with chipotle sauce and the house sauce (also a favorite)! It has two locations in Manhattan, but in my opinion, this is the best one.

BY CHLOE

185 Bleecker Street | bychefchloe.com
This vegan fast-food chain serves desserts, salads, sandwiches, ice cream, juices, and delicious food all day long! There is usually a line during lunchtime. By Chole has many locations in NY, but the one in the West Village has a Sweets By Chloe right next to it, for vegan desserts made by them as well.

LADYBIRD

111 E 7th St | www.ladybirdny.com
One of the most beautiful vegan restaurants! Most vegan restaurants use "fake meat" to prepare the dishes, in this one, the flavor comes exclusively from the vegetables - which is awesome! The restaurant has great reviews by vegan and nonvegans! Another nice thing about the Ladybird is the selection of drinks and cocktails, which are all wine-based. Prices range between $12-14 per cocktail. The menu is quite simple and the average price per dish is around $14 and $18 (2020).

JAJAJA PLANTAS MEXICANAS

162 East Broadway | www.jajajamexicana.com
If you enjoy genuine Mexican food, this is your place! JaJaJa has four locations, one in the Lower East Side, one in the West Village, one in the Hudson Yards and one in Williamsburg. They offer some gluten-free options. It is common to find a line for dinner and they don't accept reservations. If you don't like spicy food, make it clear and opt for mild dishes. Their menu is pretty long but most main dishes and starters are in the $9-16 range in 2020.

AVANT GARDEN

130 East 7th Street
Avant Garden brings rich flavor to every dish and they don't use vegan fake meats. Everything is very tasty! We ordered the Romesco toast ($14) and the Paella ($22). The atmosphere is nice, but still casual and you can sit by the kitchen counter and see the chefs bringing your orders to life.

BAREBURGER

Okay, I admit this one is a plus. It is not an exclusively vegan burger place, but 50% of their menu is vegan so I had to include it! Plus, this is the perfect spot if you are traveling with non-vegans and there are several locations in NYC and yes, they serve two of the most famous vegan burgers: Beyond Meat and The Impossible Burger.

GLUTEN-FREE (FRIENDLY) *restaurants*

Gluten-free options are very common in restaurants in New York, as well as vegetarian or vegan. So even if they don't appear on the menu, it is always worth asking if there are any special dishes available. Especially in sophisticated restaurants, the chefs often create something off the menu to accommodate customers with special diets.

NOGLU
1266 Madison Avenue - www.noglu.fr/en/english-new-york
French bakery with a fully organic and locally-sourced menu and 100% gluten-free! From traditional sandwiches, quiches and salads to pastries and sweets, it is the perfect spot for a delicious afternoon tea break or breakfast! It's also a grocery store and a take-out eatery!

SENZA GLUTEN
206 Sullivan St
This is a 100% gluten-free restaurant and probably the best one in the West Village/SoHo area!
It is a bit pricey when compared to other restaurants, the average main course cost, for example, is $30, but they are worth every penny! The desserts are in the $11-15 range.

BY CHLOE
In addition to being 100% vegan fast food, you'll also find gluten-free options on the menu that vary from salads and sandwiches to pasta, toast, and sweets.

PAPPARDELLA

316 Columbus Avenue (corner of 75th Street)
pappardella.getbento.com/#menu
For those who are passionate about Italian food, Pappardella cannot be neglected here either. It is not entirely gluten-free but it has created a super diversified menu to address the demand.

TACOMBI

tacombi.com/menu
It's a great place for a happy hour with friends, it has lots of drinks and juices as well as the experience of eating authentic Mexican food in the heart of New York in a super relaxed atmosphere! And they also offer corn-based tortillas.
Friendly advice: If you don't like spicy food make this very clear when ordering. The prices are okay, tacos cost $3.95 each.

MAREA

240 Central Park South | www.marea-nyc.com
Specialized in seafood, the sophisticated Italian restaurant Marea is located close to Central Park and offers gluten-free options for those who want to try their pasta, but still, their focus is seafood: oysters, caviar, raw fish, plus steaks and a great wine selection. They open for lunch, dinner, and brunch as well as offering a seafood tasting menu for $95 per person. The restaurant has two Michelin stars!

If you need more options, I recommend Cosme, The Little Beet Table, Dosa Royale, and as a supermarket option, I recommend Whole Foods Market and Trader Joe's! Also, make sure you download food apps such as Yelp to filter options and find gluten-free options near you.

January

D	S	T	Q	Q	S	S
		1	2	3	4	5
6	7	8	9	10	11	12
13	14	15	16	17	18	19
20	21	22	23	24	25	26
27	28	29	30	31		

1: First day of the year
21: Martin Luther King Jr. Day
Chinese New Year
End of January and beginning of February
Restaurant Week
End of January and beginning of February

14: Valentine's Day
Restaurants get very busy, make an early reservation
18: President's Day
Several stores have sales between February 12 and 22
New York Fashion Week
The 1st two weeks of February

February

D	S	T	Q	Q	S	S
					1	2
3	4	5	6	7	8	9
10	11	12	13	14	15	16
17	18	19	20	21	22	23
24	25	26	27	28		

March

D	S	T	Q	Q	S	S
					1	2
3	4	5	6	7	8	9
10	11	12	13	14	15	16
17	18	19	20	21	22	23
24	25	26	27	28	29	30
31						

17: St. Patrick's Parade
The parade takes place on 5th Avenue, beginning on 44th Street and ending on 86th Street
25: Greek Independence Day
The parade takes place on 5th Avenue, beginning on 49th Street and ending on 59th Street.

Easter Flower Show: An annual themed show hosted by Macy's
Easter Sunday Parade: The parade takes place on 5th Avenue beginning on 44th Street and ending on 59th Street.

Cherry Blossom Festival: Brooklyn Botanic Garden and New York Botanical Garden
Tribeca Film Festival
between late March and early April
New York City Ballet: The spring presentation is between April and June.
Baseball games: From late April to early October, the Yankees and Mets take the field.

April

D	S	T	Q	Q	S	S
	1	2	3	4	5	6
7	8	9	10	11	12	13
14	15	16	17	18	19	20
21	22	23	24	25	26	27
28	29	30				

May

D	S	T	Q	Q	S	S
			1	2	3	4
5	6	7	8	9	10	11
12	13	14	15	16	17	18
19	20	21	22	23	24	25
26	27	28	29	30	31	

Five Boro Bike Tour:
On the first Sunday of May, 68km are cycled with a cheerful celebration at the end.
Cuban Day parade:
First Sunday of May on 6th Avenue between 44th Street and Central Park South
Memorial Day Parade:
On the last weekend of May, the parade takes place on 5th Avenue and the celebration goes on to South Street Seaport.

June

D	S	T	Q	Q	S	S
	1	2	3	4	5	6
7	8	9	10	11	12	13
14	15	16	17	18	19	20
21	22	23	24	25	26	27
28	29	30	31			

Museum Mile Festival: On the 2nd Tuesday of the month. From 85th Street to 105th Street. Free admission between 6 pm and 9 pm to museums within the area. Learn more here: *museummilefestival.org*

Central Park Summer Stage
Between June and August, several concerts take over Central Park.
Metropolitan Opera Parks Concerts: There are several concerts in different parks around the city.
Shakespeare in the Park: Between June and September the Delacorte Theater Central Park is taken over by art.
Movie nights: several NYC parks screen movies for free mostly from June-September
NYC Pride March: The parade begins on 36th Street and goes through 5th Avenue until Christopher Street and the Stonewall Inn.
Governors Ball: Music Festival on Randall's Island

July

D	S	T	Q	Q	S	S
	1	2	3	4	5	6
7	8	9	10	11	12	13
14	15	16	17	18	19	20
21	22	23	24	25	26	27
28	29	30	31			

U.S.A. Independence Day: Fireworks light up New York's skyline. Recently, it has occured on the East River, midtown.
Mostly Mozart Festival: Between July and August at Avery Fisher Hall at Lincoln Center.
NYC Philharmonic Parks: Free concerts around town.

August

D	S	T	Q	Q	S	S
				1	2	3
4	5	6	7	8	9	10
11	12	13	14	15	16	17
18	19	20	21	22	23	24
25	26	27	28	29	30	31

US Open Tennis Championships: Between late August and early September at Flushing Meadows

September

D	S	T	Q	Q	S	S
1	2	3	4	5	6	7
8	9	10	11	12	13	14
15	16	17	18	19	20	21
22	23	24	25	26	27	28
29	30					

Brazilian Day: On the first Sunday of the month, at 46th Street and 6th Avenue.
San Gennaro Party: In the third week of September, there is a ten day celebration and lots of delicious food in Little Italy in Manhattan and Bronx.
New York Film Festival: Between the middle of September and the beginning of October.
The 1st two weeks of September: New York Fashion Week.

October

Columbus Day Parade: 2nd Monday of the month. On 5th Avenue, beginning on 44th Street and ending on 86th Street.
Rockefeller Center Ice Skating Rink: It is the first of the most famous rinks to start activities and stays open until early April.
31: Halloween Parade: It starts on 6th Avenue and Canal Street and goes up to 16th Street.
Basketball games: The basketball season starts.

D	S	T	Q	Q	S	S
		1	2	3	4	5
6	7	8	9	10	11	12
13	14	15	16	17	18	19
20	21	22	23	24	25	26
27	28	29	30	31		

November

D	S	T	Q	Q	S	S
1	2	3	4	5	6	7
8	9	10	11	12	13	14
15	16	17	18	19	20	21
22	23	24	25	26	27	28
29	30	31				

New York City Marathon: 1st Sunday of the month, the marathon runs through all five neighborhoods that make up New York City.
Macy's Thanksgiving parade: On the 4th Thursday of the month. It starts on Central Park West and 79th Street and it ends at Macy's, on 34th Street and Broadway.

December

Tree Lighting Ceremony: The Rockefeller Center tree is lit early in the month at a show that pulls out crowds and features celebrity hosts.
Santa Con: date varies, check the official website for updates: www.santacon.info/New_York-NY/
31: The most famous New Years Eve in the world!

D	S	T	Q	Q	S	S
1	2	3	4	5	6	7
8	9	10	11	12	13	14
15	16	17	18	19	20	21
22	23	24	25	26	27	28
29	30	31				

 clothes, coats, handbags, shoes and accessories with competitive prices

Burlington Coat Factory, TJ Maxx, Marshalls, Century 21, Macy's, DSW Shoes, Nordstrom Rack, Bloomingdale's Outlet

shoes

DSW Shoes, Famous Footwear, Footlocker, Century 21, Macy's, TJ Maxx, Marshalls, Nordstrom, Nordstrom Rack, Bloomingdale's and most clothing stores in general.

beauty products, perfumes, and makeup

Sephora, Harmon Face Values, Ulta Beauty, Macy's, Credo, Bloomingdale's, The Detox Market, Bed Bath & Beyond, drugstores and other department stores

electronics

B & H Photo Video, Best Buy, Adorama, Foto Care

baby clothes and needs

Buy Buy Baby, Albee Baby, The Children's Place, Marshalls, TJ Maxx, Target.

wedding dresses

David's Bridal, RK Bridal, Pronovias, Wedding Atelier, Saks, Vera Wang, Designer Loft, Monique Lulhier, Mark Ingram Atelier, Bergdorf, Kleinfeld, The One Bridal Boutique and Gabriella New York Bridal Salon.

party dresses

Macy's, Nordstrom Rack, Bloomingdale's Outlet, NYC Glamor Couture, Pronovias, stores in the Garment District, TJMaxx, Marshalls.

party supplies, DIY, scrapbooking, stationary, painting and arts and crafts in general

Michaels, Blick Art Materials, Party City, Paper Source, Dollar Tree, Village Party Store.

 discount stores

Jack's 99 Cent Store, Lot-Less, Five Below, Marshalls, TJ Maxx, Burlington, Nordstrom Rack, Bloomingdale's Outlet.

supermarkets

Whole Foods, Trader Joe's, Key Food, Fairway Market, Food Bazaar, Food Emporium, Morton Williams Supermarket, CTown Supermarket, Foodtown.

home and kitchen utensil stores

Williams-Sonoma, West Elm, Sour la Table, Fishs Eddy, TJ Maxx, Marshalls, Pottery Barn, Bed Bath and Beyond.

pharmacies

Duane Reade, Walgreens, CVS, Rite Aid.

toys

Disney Store, Five Below, FAO Schwarz, Kidding Around, Target, Forbidden Planet, Lego Store, American Girl Store, Kmart, Barnes and Noble.

perfume shops
Olfactory, Le Labo, Atelier Cologne, Sephora, Macy's, Bloomingdale's, etc.

soap and body products stores
Sabon, Lush, Bath & Body Works, Soapology, Natura Brasil, Arianna Skincare.

thrift stores
Buffalo Exchange, Crossroads Trading Company, Housing Works, Goodwill, Angel Street Thrift Shop, Vintage Thrift, INA, Beacon's Closet.

Most Popular
OUTLETS

New York is also great for shopping! But if you have a lot on your wish list and the discount stores already mentioned don't do the trick, a good option would be to explore three of the biggest outlet malls nearby. When shopping in New York state, clothing and footwear under U$110 (per item) are exempt from New York sales tax.

Happy shopping!

1 THE MILLS AT JERSEY GARDENS

651 Kapkowski Rd, Elizabeth, NJ - www.simon.com/mall/the-mills-at-jersey-gardens
This is an indoor shopping mall, so you won't have to change plans if it rains!
Directions: Bus # 111 or # 115 departing from Port Authority Bus Terminal
Schedule and more info: *www.njtransit.com*
It takes about half an hour and the round trip costs $14. You can buy the tickets at the same station machines. Ask to get off at the Jersey Gardens stop.

2 EMPIRE OUTLETS

55 Richmond Terrace, Staten Island, NY - www.empireoutlets.nyc
Great views of Manhattan and outdoor space, you can get there by taking the free Manhattan ferry to Staten Island or by bus and car.

3 WOODBURY COMMON PREMIUM OUTLETS

498 Red Apple Court, Central Valley, NY - www.premiumoutlets.com/outlet/wood-bury-common

Located about an hour from NYC, there are about 200 shops including some of the most sought-after brands. The bad thing about it is that the place is an open area shopping mall- between one store to another, you might get exposed to cold, heat or rain. You can go by bus ($30-40 on average), by car, with a private driver or by train + bus/cab ... Some bus companies offer this route.

DAY TRIPS FROM NYC

Sleepy Hollow	Bear Mountain State Park
Tarrytown	Minnewaska State park
Beacon	Southampton
Cold Spring	Hoboken
Storm King	Philadelphia
Fire Island	Washington DC (about 4 hours away)
Wineries on Long Island	

NEW YORK

WITH KIDS

Traveling with kids? I've got it covered! Here are some of the coolest things you can do with kids (besides the city itself)! Don't forget to access the blog *(www. nyandabout.com/en)* for more information:

 Museums

- NYC Transit Museum
- Children's Museum of Manhattan
- The National Museum of Natural History
- Intrepid Sea, Air and Space Museum
- Children's Museum of the Arts
- The New York City Fire Museum
- Metropolitan Museum of Art

 Parks

- Luna Park (Amusement Park)
- Central Park
- Brooklyn Bridge Park
- Domino Park
- Battery City Park
- Little Island

 Stores

- Disney Store
- American Girl Store
- Lego Store
- Dylan's Candy Bar
- Harry Potter Store
- M&M's Store
- FAO Schwarz
- Camp

 Entertainment

- Broadway Musicals like The Lion King and Aladdin
- Dave and Busters

 Restaurants

- Ellen's Stardust
- Alice's Tea Cup
- American Girl Store Cafe
- Big daddy's
- Dave and Busters
- Black Tap
- Serendipity
- Carmine's
- Junior's

 Attractions

- Roosevelt Island Tram
- Central Park Zoo
- Bronx Zoo
- SPYSCAPE
- Madame Tussaud Wax Museum
- Mini Golf at Pier 25
- And all the NYC classic spots! Kids usually love them as much as we do!

BROADWAY

There are so many ways to get Broadway tickets at a discount. I will suggest some of the most famous ones, but keep in mind that sometimes you will not be able to buy last-minute tickets for specific dates. So it is important to have some flexibility in your itinerary.

To check out what types of tickets are available for each show I suggest this website: *www.broadwayforbrokepeople.com*

TYPES OF DISCOUNT:

TKTS
Tickets with up to 50% off for performances on the same day. The line at the Times Square booth (corner of 47th and 7th Avenue) is quite long, so I recommend the one downtown, which is usually less crowded.

TODAY TIX
Similar to TKTS, *Today Tix* is another way to buy that cheap last-minute ticket (or in advance) online, without having to stand in line, so I highly recommend it! You usually can get your tickets with the *Today Tix* agents at the theater door 30 minutes prior to the show starts, they wear a company T-shirt, so it's relatively easy to find them. You'll just have to identify yourself, confirm the number of tickets you have bought, sign the receipt and enjoy the show. They do charge a fee, so make sure it is worth it. They sell tickets about thirty days in advance on the website.

BROADWAY ROULETTE
If you have no preference for a particular show, check out Broadway Roulette, you choose the day and they choose the show! Tickets are U$49-59. Visit the website here: *www.broadwayroulette.com*

STUBHUB
People buy and resell tickets on stubhub, the site is safe and sometimes you can find great deals and save a lot of money. Learn more here: *www.stubhub.com*

AT THE THEATER
You can also head straight to the ticket counter and check prices for tickets, you will be surprised how many discounted tickets may be available.

ON LOCATION LOTTERY

Available only for some shows (see which ones on *www.playbill.com*). Head to the theater 2.5 hours before the show when they hold the lottery. It goes like this: you write your name on a piece of paper and request however many tickets you would like (one or two). If you are chosen, you pay around $30 each. They usually draw 13 papers (up to 26 tickets) and the winners are announced publicly.

ONLINE LOTTERY

Another inexpensive way to try to get a great discount is by using the Broadway online lottery! To compete simply check the website on the day or the day before the show! *www.lottery.broadwaydirect.com* (some shows have their own system) If you win, you must pay your online ticket with an (international) credit card within one hour of receiving the confirmation email! If you don't pay, you'll lose the ticket.Tickets cost on average $30 - $40.

RUSH TICKET

These are last minute tickets but they start being sold as soon as the box office opens. Check out the shows that are offering rush tickets on the Playbill website then go to the booth and ask if there are any available tickets for that day.

STUDENT TICKET

Just check the playbill website to see which shows offer a student discount and head to the theater with your valid school card on a specific day and time for the purchase.

 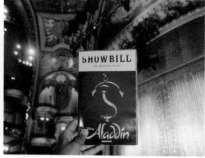

USEFUL APPS
in Nyc

LYFT, UBER AND VIA
car service applications

YELP AND ZAGAT
find restaurants and read reviews

NEW YORK SUBWAY MTA MAP
For subway map and service status

GOOGLE MAPS
what I use to guide me anywhere the city

OPEN TABLE
make restaurant reservations

CITYMAPPER
another option to navigate NY

SEAMLESS E GRUBHUB
order food online

INFATUATION
great for looking out for great restaurants for all occasions

NYC FERRY
check out the ferries that connect different parts of NYC,
check schedules and buy tickets.

SIT OR SQUAT
find restrooms near you.

SHOPDROP
For those who love to shop, find deals and the famous sample sales
that happen around the city.

CITIBIKE
find the Citi bike spots near you and buy your daily pass!

TODAY TIX E TKTS
keep an eye out and buy Broadway show tickets at a discount price

HOTEL TONIGHT
Need a last-minute hotel deal? Check this app out!

AIRBNB
To rent rooms and book experiences in NYC

HAPPY COW
To find vegan and vegetarian restaurants

SPECIAL DISCOUNTS FOR MY FOLLOWERS

in Ny

 ### Souvenirs: 5th Ave NY Gifts | 10% off

377 5th Avenue - 5th Avenue, between 35th and 36th Streets
Mention my name and get 10% off your purchase! Their prices are usually very competitive.

 ### UBER AND LYFT apps

Discount on the first time using the Uber app: **marthas188**
Discount on the first time using Lyft app: **MARTHA351616**

 ### Bag All | 20% off

219 Mott Street
The Bag All store offers a 20% discount for my readers when shopping at the store or online. Just use the code **MARTHA** code at check-out

 ### Petisco Brazuca | 10% off

833 Dekalb Avenue, Brooklyn | www.petiscobrazuca.com
Discount Code: NYandabout

 ### Face Haus | U$10 off

1140 Third Avenue | thefacehaus.com
Get 10% off any regular face treatment with my code: BlogNYAndAbout

 ### Photo shoots in NYC | U$15 off

Get $15 off your photo shoot with me with the code **NYANDABOUT15**:
www.marthasachserphotography.com

 ### Hot tub boat tour - free towel rent
Get a free towel during your ride with code MARTHA TOWELS
Insert code in the comment box when booking
www.seathecity.com

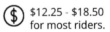

◆ JFK airport

subway + AirTrain

$ $11.50/person
($7.75 AirTrain + $2.75 subway +
U$1.00 new card fee)

🕐 50 minutes
to midtown Manhattan

After passing by the immigration officer and picking up your bags, just follow the signs to Airtrain, a train that connects the airport terminals and the subway station (lines E, Z and J).Type your destination address on the GPS/ Google Maps to check the best subway line for you.

train

$ $12.25 - $18.50
for most riders.

🕐 45 minutes to Penn Station

You can also take the Long Island Rail Road when you leave the AirTrain to Manhattan or other places (like places in Queens that aren't on the E line). They are more comfortable than the subway and the price and time vary according to the destination.

TIP: If your destination is NYC, you can save money on weekends by purchasing the **CityTicket** through the MTA eTix app and pay only $4.50 instead.

I advise you to estimate how often you will use the subway so you can decide if you should buy the unlimited subway metrocard and bus pass for 7 days ($33 +$1.00 - as in 2021).You will still need to add the $5 for the Airtrain.t

You can buy it at the station when you get off the AirTrain. The machines don't give change for larger bills, so use small bills or break it with a subway officer. It is possible to pay with a credit card. Oh! The metro card costs $1, save it so you don't have to buy it again and simply recharge when/if you need it.

You can buy your ticket at Jamaica Station using the vending machines or using the MTA eTIX app. Don't forget to buy your ticket before you board the train as it can cost you more. Check the website for more information and schedule: *www.mta.info/lirr*.

Keep in mind that, **FOR BOTH THE METRO AND THE TRAIN,** the machine will request your zip code when making a purchase with a credit card. In this case, simply enter the numbers 99999, so the machine will know that your card is from abroad.

◆ Newark International Airport

Like JFK, Newark International Airport also has an AirTrain which connects to the New Jersey Transit ($15.25 to Penn Station in Manhattan) and Amtrak, other trains that take you to Manhattan and other locations in the state/ country. NJ Transit tickets include the fare for the AirTrain. Otherwise it costs $7.75. You can also choose to take the bus route, learn more on the airport's official website. But in my opinion, the train is much faster and simpler.

boarding area

◆ shared transportation

This is a great option if you are traveling on a budget but I don't recommend if you are on a tight schedule. There are different companies that offer shared transportation but one of the most popular service is Go Airlink NYC.

Go Airlink NYC
www.goairlinkshuttle.com
Door-to-door services available 24 hours a day, 7 days per week. You can make a reservation online, there are different types of transportation services available.

Uber pool
You share the ride with others for more affordable prices. I used it once and it was quite budget-friendly, but it took much longer.

Regular Uber and Lyft are also available. Follow the signs or ask for help if you aren't sure where the pick-up locations are and which terminal you're in.

◆ taxi

Manhattan-JFK (both ways)
Flat rate of $52 (in 2021) + tip (15 to 20%)+ maybe small fees. If the driver goes through a toll, the passenger must pay for it - you can request alternative routes if you want to and if available. There is another fee that costs less than $1. If the ride is between 4 pm and 8 pm on weekdays (excluding holidays), there will be an extra charge of $4.50.

Newark International Airport
It's based on the cab's meter, not a fixed rate like JFK.

La Guardia Airport
The price is also not fixed, it varies according to the meter.

Watch out for drivers who offer rides out of the airport, they are not allowed to do this. If you decide to take a taxi, look for the yellow ones, which are usually arranged in a line waiting for passengers.

1. GOVERNOR'S ISLAND

From the military quarter to one of the greatest playgrounds for New Yorkers. It is a historical landmark accessible through the official ferry and is open to the public between May and October and different events also take place there. The view of Manhattan is beautiful and it is a great alternative for a relaxing afternoon for the entire family. You can have a picnic, ride a bike, get a tan, some drinks and snacks and enjoy the local vibe. The highlights of the island include Fort Jay, historic houses (Colonels Row), Castle Williams, Slide Hill and Hammock Grove. The ferry departs from the Battery Maritime Building and it costs $3 round trip or free on weekends before 11:30. Visit the official website for updated ferry schedule and info: *govisland.com/*

2. RED HOOK

Red Hook is one of those nice surprises in NYC! Red Hook is located in the Carroll Gardens neighborhood in Brooklyn and it went from being known as a harbor and industrial area to the city's new funky neighborhood. I believe that what makes this area so unique is the slow pace, the fact that the NYC ferry is the easiest way to get there and obviously, the beautiful views of the city. Check out the Red Hook itinerary here in the guide!

3. INDUSTRY CITY

Factories and warehouse sheds have given way to a new era for this neighborhood. Around 500,000 square meters and headquarters of several companies, eateries, shops, a Japanese village (a food hall and grocery) and year-round experiences. Industry City is a place worth adding to the itinerary if you have the time. In winter, aside from hosting the Brooklyn Flea Market on the second floor of Building 1, if you enjoy cooking, I recommend venturing into one of The Brooklyn Kitchen's classes! Right next to it is the Li-Lac chocolate factory, where you can tour as well and don't skip Japan Village, with several vendors and even a market!

4. BRONX LITTLE ITALY

I think this might be news for many people, but Little Italy in Manhattan is considered by most locals to be the Little Italy "for tourists"! For a more authentic experience head to the Bronx where you will find nice restaurants, markets and everything related to Italian cuisine which has been passed down from generation to generation.

5. CONEY ISLAND

In warmer months, Coney Island has a lot to offer to the whole family. Besides the beach and the amusement park, a pier with several food and entertainment alternatives make children of all ages really happy! It's not very close, a subway ride to midtown takes about an hour. Check out the complete itinerary here in the guide!

6. LONG ISLAND CITY

Really close to Manhattan, LIC has one of the most beautiful views of the city. With modern buildings rising up every year, the area attracts more and more young people and families in search of more space and quality of life. On July 4, Independence Day in the United States, the area draws crowds to a spectacular view of the fireworks with Manhattan in the background.

7. BUSHWICK

This area has undergone many changes throughout history. No longer just known as an industrial area, it has established an artistic and groovy atmosphere. Its greatest charm is the open wall art/murals, which are part of The Bushwick Collective and draws crowds who admire the graphite paintings on the streets of the neighborhood. There are also nice restaurants in the area.

8. ASTORIA

One of New York's most multicultural neighborhoods, you can travel around the world without leaving Astoria! The region also has a strong Greek and Italian heritage, with great restaurants and supermarkets. In nice weather, it is worth visiting Astoria Park, with a nice playground for the little ones and even a communal swimming pool with a gorgeous view of the city.

9. DOMINO PARK

Built on the Williamsburg waterfront, in front of the defunct Domino sugar factory, the park attracts tourists and locals year round. It's the perfect place to go at the end of the day during the summer. You can watch people practicing sports (such as beach volleyball !!), skateboarding, letting the kids run free at the playground while admiring the stunning view of Manhattan!

10. THE MET CLOISTERS

This is also part of the Metropolitan Museum of Art and is dedicated to art, architecture, and gardens of Medieval Europe. Would you like to feel like you are in another time and place? Add this museum to your itinerary! The museum is north of Fort Tryon Park in Uptown, on the west side, next to the Hudson River.

ROOFTOPS

On the blog *(www.nyandabout.com)* you will find several posts about rooftops in New York, but I selected some of my favorite to make it easier for you:

What you need to know before you go:

- Rooftops are generally free, but the drinks and food can be a bit more expensive than they would be in a conventional bar.

- Minors can't enter the rooftops that operate as a bar. If there is a restaurant option during the day they might enter the establishment accompanied by an adult until a certain time. Always check the official website and contact them via email or social media.

- Most of the bars listed below don't have a very formal dress code, others do. Visit the official websites or contact them via email for details.

- In the summer very often there will be a line at the door to get in. Get ready to wait for a little while.

- Bring your ID! You need to prove that you are over 21 years old to get in and buy alcohol.

- Not all rooftops have tables and chairs for everyone to sit on. As a rule, people stand, enjoy the view, chat...Some places might have a minimum charge for table reservation.

- Most rooftops also have indoor space so they can remain open year-round.

- Most rooftops usually open late in the afternoon, around 4pm.

SOME OF MY FAVORITE ROOFTOPS

- **THE SKYLARK** | 200 WEST 39TH STREET
- **MAGIC HOUR** | 485 7TH AVENUE, 18TH FLOOR
- **THE PRESS LOUNGE** | 653 11TH AVE, 16TH FLOOR
- **230 5TH** | 230 FIFTH AVENUE (ESTH OF 27TH WITH A 5TH AVE)
- **ROOF GARDEN CAFE AND MARTINI BAR (AT THE
- **METROPOLITAN MUSEUM OF ART)** | 1000 5TH AVE
- **PHD MIDTOWN** | 210 W 55TH STREET AT THE DREAM HOTEL
- **MR. PURPLE** | 180 ORCHARD STREET
- **1 ROOFTOP BAR HOTEL** | 60 FURMAN ST, BROOKLYN
- **LE BAIN** | 848 WASHINGTON STREET
- **WESTLIGHT** | 111 N 12TH STREET, 22ND FLOOR, BROOKLYN
- **DEAR IRVING ON HUDSON** | 310 W. 40TH STREET
- **GALLOW GREEN** | 542 W 27TH STREET

- TIMEOUT MARKET AND EMPIRE STORES

- PIER 17

- CANTOR ROOFTOP GARDEN BAR AT THE METROPOLITAN MUSEUM OF ART

- LOOPY DOOPY BAR AT CONRAD HOTEL

- SERRA BY BIRRERIA AT EATALY
- 230 5TH (ON WEEKENDS DURING BRUNCH HOURS, BUT I ALWAYS RECOMMEND CONTACTING THEM BEFORE TO CONFIRM)

Cheap Eats

RUDY'S BAR AND GRILL
Buy a beer (U$3) and get a free hot dog.

CROCODILE LOUNGE
Free pizza with each drink (beers start at U$5)

TWO BROS PIZZA
U$1 slice (cheese pizza)

HALAL GUYS FOOD TRUCK
W 53rd St, New York
The iconic food truck serves meals for less than U$10

BLEECKER STREET PIZZA
U$3 cheese slice

RICE ROLLS AT JOE'S STEAM RICE ROLL
wontons and dumplings. The vegetable option is U$4.

VANESSA'S DUMPLING HOUSE
Dumplings, buns and more for less than U$5!

MAMOUN'S FALAFEL
A decent size falafel wrap for less than U$5.

Treats not to miss in Nyc
THE CHECKLIST

- [ ] Joe's Pizza (if you are a Spider Man fan!)

- [ ] Rice To Riches - rice pudding

- [ ] Grilled Corn at Cafe Habana

- [ ] Roasted potatoes topped with melted raclette cheese from Raclette NYC

- [ ] Cheesecakes at Eileen's Special Cheesecake

- [ ] Waffles from Wafels and Dinges

- [ ] Titanic at Carmine's

- [ ] Hot dog from Nathan's Famous Hot Dog in Coney Island

- [ ] Rainbow bagel at the Bagel Store

- [ ] Center-filled cupcakes from Molly's Cupcakes

- [ ] Banana Pudding from Magnolia Bakery

- [ ] A scoop or 2 from OddFellows Ice Cream

- [ ] Pastrami Sandwich at Katz Delicatessen

- [ ] Any instagrammable Milkshake at Black Tap

- [ ] Chocolate Chip Walnut Cookie at Levain Bakery

- [ ] Chocolate Chunk Cookie from Insomnia Cookies

- [ ] Cronut at Dominique Ansel

- [ ] The Works at Burger Joint

INSTAGRAMMABLE SPOTS IN NYC

If you love taking pictures like me, here are some of my favorite "instagrammable spots" in the city:

MANHATTAN BRIDGE VIEW FROM BROOKLYN
If you are planning a trip to Brooklyn, this shot of the beautiful Manhattan Bridge is the most popular one! There are people all day long trying to get the perfect shot for instagram and believe me, it might take some time to get one without people in the background! How to get there? This is the corner of Washington and Water Street in DUMBO.

OCULUS
This is if not the most, one of the most expensive metro stations in the world and to me, one of the most unique when it comes to architecture, which was built to resemble a winged dove! There are countless angles for a good photo there, just get creative! The balcony is always very busy but you have to be patient, it took me about 5-10 minutes to get this shot.

CENTRAL PARK
I'm pretty sure that you will pay a visit to Central Park when in NYC but there are certain spots that make the perfect shot for the gram! Here are some of my favorites: The Pond, Cat Rock, Sheep Meadow, Bethesda Fountain and Terrace, Bowl Bridge, Belvedere Castle and Trefoil Arch.

BROOKLYN BRIDGE
There are so many angles you can explore on the bridge and once you cross to the Brooklyn side, you can get the city and the bridge in the background! The down side? The bridge is always crowded so you might need to wait a bit to take a good photo without dozens of people behind you! To avoid the crowds, I recommend shooting near the second arch, from Manhattan to Brooklyn, which is less crowded and of course, arriving super early or waiting until after sunset. But other than that, any time works, just be patient and you will be fine!

DUMBO

This is one of my favorite places in the world. I love seeing the New York skyline and the Brooklyn Bridge from there.

FLATIRON BUILDING

Located between Fifth Avenue and Broadway, when it was completed in 1902, the Flatiron building was one of the tallest buildings in the city at 20 floors high and one of the two skyscrapers of its time. You can take photos in front of it, but if you turn to the opposite side, you will face the Empire State Building, which is one of my favorite buildings in the world!

STONE STREET | FINANCIAL DISTRICT

Stone Street is located in the Financial District and it's a historic and charming cobblestone street. In the summer there are tables and benches outside, it is the perfect spot for a happy hour! In the colder months the tables aren't outside so you can take pictures with the beautiful buildings in the background.

GREENE STREET | SOHO

SoHo is a must see when visiting the city! The architecture is just so beautiful that you will find yourself snapping away. My favorite street for pictures is Greene Street, but have fun exploring as much as possible!

THE VESSEL

The Vessel is one of the most photographed spots in midtown and it is easy to see why! There are endless photo ops even though the view isn't the best NYC has to offer (head up to the Edge for more stunning views).

WEST VILLAGE

The most charming neighborhood of New York offers endless photo opportunities but my favorite streets are Perry and the intersection of Grove and Bedford (also known as the place where the Friends building is located!)

NOMO SOHO | HOTEL

If you want a picture by yourself and save some time, I recommend arriving as soon as they open it, around 8 am! You can get the basic ticket to the 86th floor or upgrade to the one with access to the 102nd floor.

EMPIRE STATE BUILDING

If you want a picture by yourself and save some time, I recommend arriving as soon as they open, around 8 am! You can get the basic ticket to the 86th floor or upgrade to the one with access to the 102nd floor.

GRAND CENTRAL TERMINAL

Inside or outside, Grand Central Terminal is a beautiful place to photograph and you might find photographers and clients snapping photos everywhere! If shooting from one of the balconies, I don't recommend the one with access to the Apple store, it is much busier.

SUBWAY STATIONS

The endless subway stations in NYC aren't the cleanest or the best in the world but they make for great photos! Get creative and have fun even when locals look mad at you for turning the station into a photo studio! Obviously, try not to block the stairs too much!

BUSHWICK

Once known as Brooklyn's industrial area, Bushwick became the place to escape the buzz of the city. The highlight of the neighborhood is definitely the graffiti and street art you will find by walking around the area, part of The Bushwick Collective. If you're feeling hungry, there are plenty of options around. For pizza head to Roberta's (261 Moore Street, Brooklyn, NY, US), for coffee, Little Skips (941 Willoughby Avenue, Brooklyn, NY, USA). There is also an Artichoke Pizza, Tres Hermanos and many more. To get there take the L train to Jefferson Street or Morgan Avenue. In the summer months when it is too humid bring a hat if you can, there aren't many trees and shaded areas around.

HIGH LINE PARK

The High Line Park is a must when visiting NYC. You can access it from different streets, but I recommend going from the 23rd towards 14th Street if you want to end your trip at Chelsea Market or from 23rd to 34th Street, to end your walk at the Hudson Yards or simply walk the entire park, it is worth it and you will find many photo opportunities! The amphitheater with a viewpoint is located above 10th avenue and 17th Street.

LONG ISLAND CITY

This is my favorite place in Queens and one that not so many people know about. The skyline of midtown feels closer than other places in the city and there are countless restaurants in the area. Plus, the neighborhood is changing so much, new buildings rising every day and a different atmosphere of NYC is in Long Island City waiting for you!

LUNA PARK

This traditional amusement park with iconic and vintage vibes is a must see! The boardwalk is also very popular, there are countless spots for snacks, ice cream and the famous Nathan's Hot Dog. Also, the New York Aquarium is right there! On Friday nights there is a firework show around 9pm on the beach, perfect way to end the day in NYC, right?

SUNDAY

"Practically everybody in New York has half a mind to write a book — and does."

Groucho Marx

I believe everyone comes to NYC eager to see the main sight-seeing areas and attractions up close in person. So to set the tone, let's devote the first day to the can't miss spots that make you feel that you have truly landed in the city that never sleeps.

 Today, **Queens Botanical Gardens** is free between 9am and 11am
43-50 Main St | queensbotanical.org

HOW TO GET THERE

🚆 5th Avenue-59th street

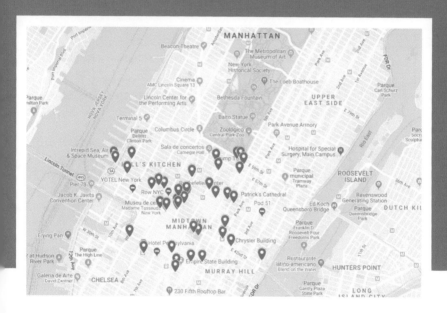

SUGGESTED BREAKFAST (OR LUNCH)

• **The Plaza Food Hall**
Fifth Avenue and Central Park South - in the basement of The Plaza Hotel

• **Burger Joint**
119 West 56thStreet - inside the Le Parker Meridien Hotel

1 5TH AVENUE

From the subway, you should get off at 60th Street, by Central Park and **Apple Store**, this is the one that is open 24 hours!

Across the street, you will see **Grand Army Plaza** with the famous **Pulitzer Fountain**, which inspired the fountain in the opening of *F.R.I.E.N.D.S.* and it was also featured on TV shows such as *Gossip Girl* and *Sex and The City*.

Across the street, you will see the historic **Plaza Hote**l, where movies like *Home Alone 2, Bride Wars, Eloise at the Plaza, American Hustle, Crocodile Dundee*, and many more have been filmed. Next to it is **Central Park**, but resist the temptation, we have a day dedicated to it later on (check Monday's itinerary)

2

After taking all the photos you want, it's time to explore the glamorous 5th Avenue. There you will find flagship stores for luxury brands (Tiffany & Co. - from the movie *Breakfast at Tiffany's* - Chanel, Gucci, Armani, Prada, Rolex, etc.) and also more popular brands (Sephora, Uniqlo, Zara, Victoria's Secret, Urban Outfitters, etc).

GOSSIP GIRL ALERT

If you are a fan of the show, walk to Madison Avenue between 50th and 51st Streets, where you'll find the famous **The Lotte Palace Hotel**, home to most of the characters in the show!
• *455 Madison Avenue*

3 Back on 5th Avenue, at the corner of 51st Street, you will find the famous **St. Patrick's Cathedral**, one of the largest Catholic churches in the USA, built in Gothic style between 1958 and 1978. The cathedral contrasts with the modern buildings around it and the vibrant energy of the city!

> **DID YOU KNOW?**
> Fifth Avenue stretches from 143rd street (in Harlem) all the way down to Washington Square Park in the Greenwich Village. It's known as one of the most expensive places to shop in the world but as you can see, It is very long so only part of It is actually surrounded by high end stores. If you wish to shop "in style", you will find most of them near Central Park, mainly between 48th and 59th Street. If you are looking for more stores, make sure to walk one block over and explore Madison Avenue, most shops are located between 57th and 72nd Street.

4 On the other side, you'll see **Rockefeller Center**, a complex of buildings between 5th and 6th Avenue, and its tallest building, the Comcast Building, located at 30 Rockefeller Plaza, is 266 meters high and it has almost 70 floors. It was constructed during the Great Depression in the 1930s and the idea behind it was to be "a city within a city". The famous **Top Of The Rock** observatory is located there with a beautiful 360-degree view of the city, overlooking the **Empire State Building** and **Central Park.** You can buy your ticket on the official website for $32-38 (2020), on the spot or through the blog! It is also included with some discount passes.

EXTRA TIP !!!!

To enjoy the view of 5th Avenue and have some drinks, the **Salon de Ning** is a rooftop bar in the Peninsula Hotel - at the corner of *5th Avenue and 55th Street*. Not as big or trendy as the other ones but worth visiting if you have time.

TIP

MoMA *(11 W 53rd St)*, the Museum of Modern Art is around the area. Admission is free on Fridays between 4 pm and 8 pm, but it is usually more crowded, of course.

TIP

If you enjoy a happy hour or dinner with a breathtaking view, on the 65th floor of the Rockefeller Center (30 Rockefeller Plaza) there is the **Rainbow Room** and the **Bar SixtyFive**. The second is perfect for a happy hour, especially during sunset ($$$ - $$$$). Since you are around, at the **NBC Experience Store** you can book a tour of the NBC studios ($ 33 per adult). In the winter, you'll find Rockefeller Center's famous ice skating rink and the giant Christmas tree that made me fall in love with NY in the movie Home Alone 2! You will also find many shops and restaurants in the area, including FAO Schwarz, NYC's most beloved toy store. The interactive piano on the second floor is a classic and became very popular after appearing in a scene from the movie BIG with Tom Hanks in 1988.

5 Take a photo in front of the iconic **Radio City Music Hall** *(1260 6th Ave)* on 6th Avenue and 50th Street, one of NY's beloved music venues. Between November and the first week of January, don't miss the amazing Christmas Spectacular show with the famous Rockettes! I recommend it especially if you are traveling with kids!

 WHERE TO EAT

The Rockefeller Center area is very commercial, so there is no shortage of options. On the first floor of the Comcast building and in the basement, you will find a variety of shops and restaurants at all prices. On the streets nearby, the famous food trucks with the best street food style are yummy and quite cheap ($5-10).

LET'S GET BACK TO 5TH AVENUE OR 6TH AVENUE

6 Go down on 5th or 6th Avenue towards 42nd Street and turn left to go to the **Grand Central Terminal**, which is at 42nd Street and Park Avenue. On the way, you can also get a view of the famous **Chrysler Building** (405 Lexington Ave - considered for almost a year the tallest building in the world until the arrival of the Empire State Building in 1931). And next to the Terminal you will also pass **One Vanderbilt**, a 77-story commercial building, one of the tallest in the city and where the Summit observatory is located, scheduled to open to the public in October 2021. **PS:** When you turn left at 42 you will pass by the **New York Public Library** and **Bryant Park**, feel free to stop for both on the way or on the way back!

7 Inside **Grand Central** the energy is unique! The ceiling is an attraction on its own and shows the 12 constellations of the Zodiac with gold-plated painting!. Another interesting fact? Look for a dark brick on the ceiling. It was kept to show what the roof's dirt was like (part of it due to the fact that you could smoke inside the station in the past) before a major restoration in the 90s. The terminal has more than 60 stores, from **Banana Republic** and **Apple Store** to a market and a sample of the **New York Transit Museum**! Be sure to check out the **Whispering Gallery**, outside the **Oyster Bar & Restaurant**. If you are traveling with someone, stay at opposite corners of the arch and say something facing the wall. You will see the sound "travel" to the other side and the other person will hear clearly even with all the noise from the station. Even if you are traveling alone, chances are you will see people stuck to the wall doing this experience, maybe you can make friends and try it, it's fun!

🔔 WHERE TO EAT

The Grand Central Oyster Bar & restaurant ($$$) has amazing seafood options and the **Cipriani Dolci** ($$$), has a nice view of the station. Make reservations in advance! For drinks in a more sophisticated environment, **The Campbell Bar** ($$$) is a good option.

You can also find the food court in the basement ($) with more affordable options such as **Shake Shack**, **Magnolia Bakery** and many others. Not far from here is the **Urbanspace Vanderbilt** (230 Park Avenue), another great food hall with plenty of food options, from Japanese to Mexican tacos!

There is also the iconic **Pershing Square** ($$), a restaurant across the street from the Terminal. The menu is quite varied. It appeared in a scene from the movie "Friends with Benefits" with Justin Timberlake and Mila Kunis. *(90 E 42nd Street)*.

8 Also, not far from there you will find the **United Nations (UN) headquarters**, between 42-48 Street and 1st Avenue. If you wish to enter and book a guided tour, visit the official website. There are several tours daily during the week and they are usually one hour long. There are no tours on weekends. *visit.un.org/content/ tickets-1*

9 Now head back to the beautiful **New York City Public Library**, another landmark of the city. The Rose Main Reading Room is a must visit! Explore the building or make sure to take at least one photo in front of it. There is a free guided tour at 11 am and 2 pm from Monday to Saturday and 2 pm on Sundays. There is public wi-fi and also bathrooms there! Enjoy!

10 Now it is time to head to **Bryant Park,** right next to the Library, a green area in the middle of midtown. If you're traveling in the summer months, the park offers several activities for the entire family such as free movie nights, game tables, carousels, reading area, mini golf, etc. In the winter, a small village appears with food options, craft shops, and the famous ice-skating rink. Across the street you will find Whole Foods, an organic grocery store that also sells fresh meals (1095 6th Ave). For dessert, there is a Waffle and Dinges at the corner of 42nd Street and 6th Avenue.

TIP

If you have free time today or another day, the **Hudson Yards**, a complex of commercial (there is even a shopping mall) and residential buildings also offers two fun experiences: **The Vessel** and the **Edge**! It is best to get tickets in advance online ($10) for The Vessel. After a few tragic incidents, visitors are no longer allowed to enter alone, you must have someone with you (last update: 06/21). You can also visit **The Edge,** the highest outdoor sky deck in the Western Hemisphere. You can buy tickets online or at the Beyond the Edge store. For an upscale dining experience, **Peak** is a restaurant located on the 101st floor, and it is a great option for a romantic dinner. Make reservations ahead of time. One block from there you will find a great **Whole Foods** with outdoot seating. Great to take a break!

11 From there, walk down Sixth Avenue to 34th Street. This is another commercial hub of the city, however the most famous spot is undoubtedly the **Empire State Building**, with 102 floors and an observatory with a 360° view of the City. Fun fact: did you know it was built in only 13 months? From March 1930 until May 1931!

TIP

To avoid lines, try to visit the Empire State Building as soon as they open (8AM) or later at night (they close at 2AM!). Keep in mind that there are fun and interactive experiences before you go up, so I recommend allocating at least 1 hour to explore it (plus waiting in line for tickets and to go up and down).

If you want to buy **NY souvenirs** in the area, I recommend the 5th Ave NY Gifts which has great prices! And by mentioning my name at check-out you get a 10% discount. It is located at 377 5th Avenue, between 35th and 36th Streets.

At the intersection of Broadway, 6th Avenue, and 34th Street, there is the famous **Herald Square,** named after the New York Herald, once published there. This is where you will find stores like Macy's, H&M, Sephora and others forming one of the city's busiest sections.

12 Since you are nearby, I suggest a trip to **Koreatown** on 32nd street. During the day, it is as busy as any other street in the area, but at night and on weekends it gets more lively, it's trendy, jammed with bars, karaoke and incredible restaurants. There are about 100 commercial establishments, so if you enjoy the Korean culture you will surely have plenty to see around here!

TIP

For those who like Korean makeup and products, Koreatown has a large selection of K-Beauty stores: The Face Shop, Kosette and others will make you happy. They are mostly located on 32nd Street, between 6th Avenue and Madison.

 WHERE TO EAT

Five Senses - $$
9 West 32nd Street
It serves traditional Korean food in a casual vibe. It is common to get free traditional appetizers when you order food.

Kang Ho Dong Baekjeong - $$$
1 East 32nd Street
This is another famous restaurant that serves Korean barbecue made with high-quality meats. Each table has its own grill, so it's a great option for an evening out with friends or for happy hour.

New Wonjo - $$
23 West 32nd Street
The specialty here is the authentic Korean BBQ! Eat upstairs where the meats are grilled over charcoal at your own table, making the experience even more special.

Hangawi - $$$
12 East 32nd Street
This is a classic Korean restaurant where you sit on cushions and take off your shoes. It serves vegetarian and vegan dishes and the food is slightly more expensive if compared to other restaurants in the area, but it is still worth it!

Her name is Han - $$
17 E 31st Street
Typical Korean dishes like noodles, barbecue and drinks.

Grace Street $-$$
17 W 32nd Street
Lattes, coffee and delicious desserts at a nice place to hang out with friends

13 Now head to 7th Avenue and see the giant **Pennsylvania Station** (the entrance on 33rd Street and 7th Avenue is beautiful) and **Madison Square Garden**, the world's most famous arena where many important concerts and games take place. You can also book the All Access Tour to learn and see more of what happens in the backstage of games and concerts.

14 When the day comes to an end, head to 42nd Street and walk around **Times Square** and finish the day there!

 SUGGESTION!

What to do/see at the Times on your first time in NY:

See a Broadway show, eat in one of the restaurants, explore the many shops and even catch a movie or go bowling.

TIP

Head west! If you are interested and have the time, especially in the summer months, I recommend including some of these spots in your itinerary:

Intrepid Sea, Air & Space Museum
Pier 86, W 46th St | www.intrepidmuseum.org
An interactive and very interesting museum dedicated to aerial, space, military and maritime history. Its collection includes the Growler submarine, the space rocket Enterprise, the Intrepid ship, and the Alpha Delta G-BOAD aircraft. $33 per adult (It is included in some discount passes).

The Press Lounge
653 11th Avenue | www.thepresslounge.com
A rooftop bar at the top of the Ink48 hotel offering a 360-degree view of the city and the Hudson River.

Gotham West Market
600 11th Ave | gothamwestmarket.com
A nice food hall (and a good alternative to take a break and enjoy the view!).

15 How about ending the day at a rooftop bar? These are some of my favorites in the Times Square area:

The Skylark
200 W 39th Street (30th floor)

Magic Hour Rooftop Bar and Lounge
485 7th Avenue (eighteenth floor)

Monarch Rooftop
71 W 35th Street (eighteenth floor)

PHD Terrace - Dream Midtown Hotel
210 W 55th Street (16th floor)

🕵️ DID YOU KNOW?

The area known as Times Square was originally called Longacre Square and only changed its name when **The New York Times** moved its headquarters to the area. Powerful, right? After some time, the place turned out to be too small for the company and they moved from there. Today, the newspaper's headquarters is located at 620 Eighth Avenue between 40th and 41st Street, in front of the Port Authority bus and subway station.

Since 2011, smoking has been prohibited in the heart of Times Square.

One of America's most-watched morning TV shows, **Good Morning America,** has a live broadcast from their studio in the heart of Times Square and you might be able to see and even meet some famous guests. For the most passionate fans, check the official website to get tickets for some live performances that might be happening at the time of your visit. The studio is on Broadway and 44th Street in Times Square. OH! MTV also has its headquarters there! (*1515 Broadway*).

Spot famous characters and iconic figures at Times Square such as *The Naked Cowboy* and different versions of the Statue of Liberty posing for pictures with tourists in exchange for tips. Pay what you think is fair. $1 is usually alright (per character)

Times Square is one of New York's most used locations in movies and TV! Have you seen any of these movies and show?
• Vanilla Sky, Enchanted, Friends With Benefits, Birdman, The Amazing Spider-Man, Teenage Mutant Ninja Turtles, August Rush, King Kong, Unbreakable Kimmy, Gossip Girl, I am Legend.

🍽️ WHERE TO EAT

Many New Yorkers refuse to have a meal in the heart of **Times Square** because they consider the food there not as good as the other amazing gastronomic options that New York has to offer and I agree. But as I said, today is the day to get into the tourist mood, and I know you won't resist! In most places, you might have to wait for a table, especially on weekends or evenings. If you want something less touristy head to 46th Street (between 7th and 9th Avenue) and go up or down 8th or 9th Avenue for other great options! But here are some Times Square places you might like:

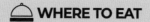
Ellen's Stardust - $ to $$
1650 Broadway
My favorite restaurant! In this old style American diner, the servers perform songs while you eat and the restaurant closes quite late, so you can finish your day there! The food is average, nothing crazy, but I love the vibe! There is usually a long line.

Olive Garden - $$
2 Times Square
Chain restaurant serving Italian food and quite affordable. Ask if there are any specials going on.

Bubba Gump - $$
1501 Broadway
Seafood is what they are most famous for and the memorabilia and pictures from the movie Forrest Gump, of course.

Dallas BBQ - $$
241 West 42nd Street
Typical Southern food! Meats, giant drinks, and relatively inexpensive dishes.

The View - $$ to $$$$
1535 Broadway
Panoramic restaurant on top of the Marriott Hotel. The experience is very nice, but the food from the buffet is ordinary.

Carmine's - $$
200 West 44th Street
Good Italian family size dishes!

Dave and Buster's - $$
234 West 42nd Street
American food, a fun game environment! Perfect for families with children.

Bareburger - $$
1515 Broadway
Delicious and nontraditional sandwiches. All organic and they also offer vegetarian and vegan options.

Rudy's Bar and Grill - $
627 9th Avenue
Cheap beer and you get a hot dog when you buy a drink. Yep, FREE!

Carlo's Bakery - Cake Boss - $
625 8th Avenue
If you are a fan, this is where you find the famous cannolis from the reality show!

Planet Hollywood - $$
1540 Broadway
Traditional American food. Perfect if you love the entertainment world.

Hard Rock Cafe - $$
1501 Broadway
Classic American food in a rock 'n' roll themed restaurant.

If you want a more sophisticated dining experience, I recommend two restaurants not too far away:

The Polo Bar (Ralph Lauren Restaurant)
$$$$ - *1 E 55th Street*
Classic, luxurious and the food is tasty.

TAO - Uptown
$$$ - *42 E 58th Street*
The decor is incredible and the menu offers a bit of Japanese, Thai and Chinese cuisine with impeccable presentation and flavor.

La Grande Boucherie
$$$- 145 W 53rd Street
French restaurant, great food and beautiful decor that will "take you" to Paris!

MONDAY

"Some might call this a fustercluck. But on the Upper East Side, we call it Sunday afternoon."

Gossip Girl

Now let's slow down a bit! Today we will explore the Upper East Side, the MET and the most famous park in the world: Central Park.

■ Take the subway 4, 5 or 6 and get off at 86 Street station. There is nothing too touristy about it, but it will give you another view of the city at a more local pace. I love watching New Yorkers running to catch the train in the morning or stopping for coffee on their way to work... Just like in the movies!

📍 HOW TO GET THERE

 Take Subway (4), (5) or (6) and get off at **86 Street**.

SUGGESTED BREAKFAST (OR LUNCH)

Bocado Cafe
1293 Lexington Avenue

Levain Bakery
1484 3rd Avenue

Le Pain Quotidien
1309 Lexington Avenue

TIP

If you have food restrictions, there is also a **Whole Foods** market nearby, with plenty of gluten-free, vegetarian and vegan options to go.
- *1551 3rd Ave,
  between 87th and 88th Street.*

I love this area because there are stores like Sephora, H&M, Barnes and Noble, It's Sugar, Best Buy, Ulta Beauty and many others. The best thing about it? They are generally less crowded than other parts of the city.

2 If it's near lunchtime, for a quick bite I suggest stopping at **Papaya King** *(179 East 86th Street)* which has one of NY's tastiest and cheapest hot dogs or maybe a stop at Shake Shack? It is located at 154 E 86th Street. If you like cookies, I recommend **Levain Bakery** nearby *(1484 3rd Ave)*.

3 From there, walk on 86th Street towards the Metropolitan Museum of Art. On the way, you will cross Park Avenue and Madison, two famous New York avenues that are very quiet and you can see their contrast with Lexington Avenue, which is super busy and full of shops. Park Avenue on the Upper East Side is residential and is one of the most expensive places to live!

GOSSIP GIRL ALERT

The Upper East Side features numerous locations used in the Gossip Girl series. Some of them are nearby:
» **Blair Waldorf Apartment:** *1136 5th Avenue, between 94th and 95th Street.*
» **Archibald Townhouse:** *4 East 74th Street, between Madison and 5th Avenue.*
» **Museum of the City of New York:** The exterior of the building was the setting for the Constance and St. Jude schools. *1220 Fifth Avenue, the corner between 103rd and 104th Street.*
» **St. James Church:** The church where Blair and Louis got married. *865 Madison Ave between 71st and 72nd Street | www.stjames.org*

TIP

For those who have more time, I recommend exploring **Carl Schurz Park!** It has a local vibe plus a beautiful view of the East River. It is on *East End Avenue, between 84th and 90th Street.*

AH! If you are a fan of the **YOU** series, the **Logos Bookstore** (called Mooney's on the show) is located at *1575 York Avenue*, close to the park.

Walk to the **Metropolitan Museum of Art (the MET)** (1000 5th Ave), one of the most famous art museums in the world. That's also where the glamorous annual MET Gala takes place and became extra famous after being used in several scenes of the Gossip Girl show! The museum also became even more popular after the movie Ocean's 8. If you are an art lover, I recommend spending at least a couple of hours inside. The museum is huge! Admission costs $25 for adults, $17 for people over 65, $12 for students and free for children under 12. Many attraction passes such as CityPASS include The MET and other museums so look at the different pass options.

TIP

At the museum, enjoy the **Roof Garden Café and Martini Bar**, with an amazing view of the city (open seasonally, Mid-April through October - weather permitting). You can get there via the elevator in the European Sculpture and Decorative Arts galleries. The rooftop bar is located on the 5th floor. Ask for directions if you need help finding it.

 If you are still in the mood for visiting museums, I highly recommend the **Guggenheim Museum** (*1071 5th Avenue | www.guggenheim.org*)! It is closed on Thursdays and you probably won't get to see everything in one short visit. It's $25 per adult, $18 for students and customers over 65. Children under 12 are free. They also offer the possibility of admissions with a suggested price on Saturdays from 5 pm to 7:45 pm, which means that you pay as much as or whatever you wish.

TIP
The Museum Mile is here and there are also several art galleries in the area! Some Suggestions:
- **Neue Galerie**: *1048 5th Avenue*
- **Michael Werner Gallery**: *4 East 77th Street*
- **Half Gallery**: *43 East 78th Street*
- **Acquavella Galleries**: *18 East 79th Street*

 WHERE TO EAT

Sant Ambroeus - $$$
1000 Madison Ave
A casual italian restaurant with multiple locations in NYC

Café Sabarsky - $$
1048 5th Avenue
Austrian style coffee serving sweet and savory delicacies.

Ralph's Coffee
888 Madison Avenue
Beautiful Ralph Lauren coffee shop

Sistina - $$$
24 E 81st Street
Upscale italian restaurant.

Serafina - $$
1022 Madison Ave
Italian restaurant serving pizzas and very tasty pasta.

Ladurée - $-$$
864 Madison Avenue
They are famous for their macarons but you will also find salads, quiches, croissants and other French delicacies.

6

From there, head over to **Central Park** and enjoy the day exploring the famous spots that have been used as backdrops in many movies and series: Bethesda Fountain, Bethesda Terrace, The Lake, The Bow Bridge, The Mall, Gapstow Bridge, Loeb Boathouse, Strawberry Fields, Sheep Meadow, Belvedere Castle, Shakespeare Garden, Jacqueline Kennedy Reservoir, Alice in Wonderland statue, Cat Rock, The Dairy (visitor center), Conservatory Garden and the Wollman Rink (winter skating rink and Victorian Gardens, amusement park for kids in spring and summer). Simply use any GPS to find the locations or check the last pages of this book for Google Maps ready links!

TIP

For those interested in Asian culture, the **Asia Society** *(725 Park Ave, between 70th and 71st Street)* is not too far. The focus is to educate people about Asia and strengthen relations between the Asian and American communities. They offer lectures, courses, exhibitions, and other cool events throughout the year.

TIP

If you love unique bookstores, **Albertine** is located on 5th Avenue and 79th Street (972 5th Avenue). Specializing in French and English books, it has a cozy reading room on the second floor with a spectacular ceiling! At the entrance, there is a replica of Michelangelo and a Venetian room.

- There is also the famous Central Park Zoo and Tisch Children's Zoo for the little ones. Tickets cost U$13.95 for adults and U$8.95 for children ages 3-12.

- If you feel like having lunch in Central Park, I recommend **Tavern on The green** ($$$) or **The Loeb Boathouse Central Par**k ($$$). It is more about the experience than the food! A bonus, both have appeared in movies such as When Harry Met Sally, Three Men and a Little Lady, Sex and The City, Ghostbusters, among others.

■ If you have more time, come back another day and rent a bike (online or on the spot)! Do some research. Prices vary according to the package and hours needed. The unlimited daily pass for Citi bikes for example cost $15, but you need to renew the rental every 30 minutes. Different companies offer a day pass outside the park near 5th Avenue and Columbus Circle.

TIP

Take free (or paid) tours around the park, focusing on its specific areas. Make your reservation in advance through the park's official website: www.centralparknyc.org/tours/

TIP

Between April and November you can rent a rowboat outside The Loeb Boathouse restaurant. The cost is $ 20 per hour (cash only), the boats accommodate up to 4 people. They charge a $ 20 returnable deposit.

7 Exit the park on *59th Street and 5th Avenue*. You'll notice that's where we started our itinerary yesterday!

8 From the park, head towards *Lexington Avenue and 59th Street*. You'll find one of NY's most famous department stores: **Bloomingdale's**. Luxury and popular clothing, beauty and accessory brands. Also, their restrooms are nice and clean.

■ The Lexington and 59th Street area is packed with stores like Sephora, Muji, H & M, Zara, and many more.

9 Before the sun does down, I suggest riding the Roosevelt Island tram, an affordable way to see the city from above, taking you to the island that sits between Queens and Manhattan. The unlimited metro card works for the tram as well but if you don't have one, the ride costs U$2.75 + U$1.00 for the metro card! Follow 59th Street east to 1st Avenue and you will find the tram station.

TIP

Aside the glamour of 5th Avenue, Madison Avenue is also a must-stop for anyone who wants to see more of the world's most famous designer brands such as Hermès, Tom Ford, Valentino, Michael Kors, Ralph Lauren, Chloé, Dolce and Gabbana, and many others!

10 If you have the energy, enjoy the evening watching a Broadway show, a jazz performance in the West Village (check the itinerary for suggestions) or maybe go shopping!

TIP

Have a sweet tooth? **Dylan's Candy Bar store** (*1011 3rd Ave*) is across the street! There is a cafe serving food and dessert options and a bar full of creative drinks. Or simply stop by for great chocolate, popular and vintage candy and ice cream. There is also a good selection of souvenirs.

🍽 WHERE TO EAT

Gina Mexicana - $$
145 E 61st St
A fine Mexican restaurant in the bustling Lexington area!

LAVO - $$$
39 East 58th Street
This sophisticated Italian restaurant and nightclub has a well varied menu: pasta, seafood, salads, and steaks. From Thursday - Sunday there are fun parties and events if you are looking for a night out or a fun brunch! Check the website for the event calendar and reservations.

Jackson Hole - $ to $$
232 East 64th Street
The place for anyone who wants a great burger at a reasonable price.

Alice's Tea Cup - $ to $$
156 East 64th Street
A teahouse inspired by the world of Alice in Wonderland. They serve teas, cakes, cookies, sandwiches... And if you love sweets like me I recommend the chocolate chip cookie and the banana cake with Nutella!

Serendipity 3 - $ to $$
225 East 60th Street
The restaurant has become even more famous since appearing in the movie Serendipity and of course for the many celeb customers.

P.J. Clarke's - $$ to $$$$
915 3rd Avenue
Hamburgers, seafood, beer and lots of history! In operation since 1884, the salon was also frequented by Frank Sinatra, Ted, and Jackie Kennedy!

On the Upper East Side, you will find museums, cultural and religious centers and much more. Remember to visit the official websites to check out hours of operation, tickets and more information:

Cooper Hewitt Smithsonian Design Museum
2 E 91st Street | www.cooperhewitt.org
Fine art exhibitions and objects. Be sure to visit the *Arthur Ross Terrace and Garden*, open to the public at no cost.

Jewish Museum
1109 5th Avenue | thejewishmuseum.org
One of the largest collections of Jewish objects, art, and history from all over the world. It's paid but it is free on Saturdays and you pay what you wish on Thursdays, between 5 pm and 8 pm.

Ukrainian Institute
2 E 79th Street | ukrainianinstitute.org
A cultural and art center dedicated with exhibitions by Ukrainian artists.

Temple Emanu-El
1 E 65th St | www.emanuelnyc.org
One of the biggest synagogues in the world.

9/11 Museum
180 Greenwich St | www.911memorial.org/museum
The museum is free to enter from 3:30 pm to 4 pm. You need to make a reservation online starting at 7am on Mondays or try in person at 3:30 pm.

TUESDAY

"New York is the meeting place of the peoples, the only city where you can hardly find a typical American."

Djuna Barnes

TIP

For those traveling with children, in front of **Café Lalo**, you will find the famous **Children's Museum of Manhattan** *(212 W 83rd Street)*! $15 per adult or child, $12 for those over 65 and free for children one year and under. There are different rooms with activities, games, toys, and exhibitions.

HOW TO GET THERE

Take Subway **1** **B** **C** to the **86th Street** stop or get off at a stop before if you want to skip the breakfast suggestions.

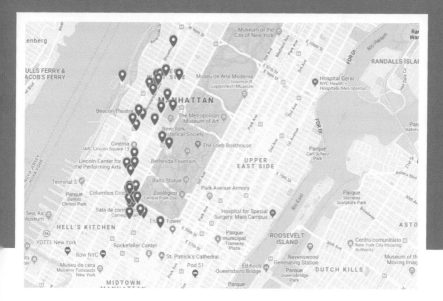

SUGGESTED BREAKFAST (OR LUNCH)

• **Café Lalo**
201 West 83rd Street
You might recognize it from the movie *You've Got Mail*

• **Good enough to eat**
520 Columbus Avenue
A classic for brunch in the area

• **Sarabeth's**
423 Amsterdam Ave
A classic for brunch & dessert in the city.

• **Modern Bread and Bagel**
472 Columbus Avenue
A gluten-free bakery!

TIP

At **Westsider Rare & Used Books** (*2246 Broadway*), you'll find used books of all kinds, vinyl records, and VHS tapes that go from floor to ceiling!

1 AFTER RECHARGING YOUR BATTERIES

The day starts at the **American Museum of Natural History** (*Central Park West and 79th Street*), one of the most famous museums in the world and great for those traveling with children. It was also featured in the famous movie Night at the Museum - although most of the movie was shot elsewhere. The museum entrance is (pay what you wish) for residents of NY, NJ and CT. General admission: $28 for adults, $16.50 for children ages 3-12, and $22.50 for students and people over 65. Special exhibitions are not included in the regular entrance. There are a few places to eat inside the museum if you need to grab a quick snack. Here are some places I recommend visiting at the museum: Milstein Hall of Ocean Life, Bernard Family Hall of North American Mammals, Akeley Hall of African Mammals, Dinosaurs, Rose Center for Earth and Space, The Discovery Room.

TIP

In the mood for good drinks? The Dead Poet (450 Amsterdam Ave # 1 between 81st and 82nd Street) is a pub created by an English teacher to celebrate the lives of famous writers and their works and offers drinks bearing their names.

Take at least 2 hours to explore the museum. Try to go early to avoid lines! The side entrance on 77th Street is generally less crowded.

DID YOU KNOW?

The **American Museum of Natural History** has a sleepover party for those who would like to spend the night there! It costs $150 per child and includes activities, snacks, and even breakfast! Kids love it! More information on the official website.

■ The **Riverside Park** starts on 72nd Street and continues for 4 miles to 158th Street along the Hudson River. Besides the wonderful view, you will find several playgrounds for children! The Hippo Playground (91st Street and Riverside Drive) is one of the kids' favorites in the summer! Several scenes from "You've Got Mail" were shot in this neighborhood.

■ On 74th Street, you will find **Levain Bakery** *(167 West 74th Street)* home of one of NY's most famous cookies! If you are not hungry, take it to go!

▷ TV SHOW TIP

If you are a fan of the **Seinfeld** series, Tom's Restaurant, a classic diner that appeared on the series, is not so close but you can walk - or take the subway. *2880 Broadway, corner of 112th Street.* Another place that appeared on the show was Gray's Papaya *(2090 Broadway, on the corner of 72nd Street)*, a fast-food restaurant famous for its cheap hot dog.

shopping

■ In the area you will also find a **Housing Works** *(306 Columbus Ave between 74th and 75th street)*, a network of thrift stores with a little bit of everything from designer pieces, accessories and home furniture.

■ Did someone say shopping? There's also a nice **Bloomingdale's Outlet** *(2085 Broadway)* at *72nd Street and Broadway*. You will find clothes, shoes, and accessories for a lower price.

2 After leaving the museum, head south on Central Park West, and let's do a quick stop at **The Dakota Building** *(1 West 72nd Street)*, famous for being John Lennon's home from 1973 to 1980, and where he was murdered.

The **Dakota** is part of the **Central Park West Historic District**, which includes other landmarks of the city such as The Majestic, Langham and San Remo, which were built between the late 19th century and 1940. You can see them side-by-side from afar on the Bow Bridge in Central Park.

🔔 WHERE TO EAT

Shake Shack - $ to $$
366 Columbus Ave

The Mermaid Inn - $$$
570 Amsterdam Ave

Peacefood Café - $ to $$
460 Amsterdam Ave

Carmine's - $$
2450 Broadway

Jean – Georges - $$$$
Trump International Hotel & Tower

Amorino - $
414 Amsterdam Ave

Café Frida - $$
368 Columbus Ave

3 Cross the street and back to the park, you'll find the iconic **Strawberry Fields** (the area between 71st and 74th street) and the mosaic with the word Imagine in the center of it. Hundreds of fans visit this memorial every day to honor John Lennon and his most famous song.

4 Now, we will walk down on Broadway, stop by the iconic **Beacon Theater** *(2124 Broadway)*, inaugurated in 1929 and the venue where stars such as Michael Jackson and the Rolling Stones have performed. On the outside, it seems like no big deal, but inside, the place has been beautifully preserved. Also take a look at the architecture of the buildings around it: New York is such a perfect mix of history and different architectural styles!

5 Let's continue our journey to the **Lincoln Center for the Performing Arts**, where the famous New York Philharmonic, the Metropolitan Opera and the New York City Ballet perform. For schedules and presentations, check out *www. lincolncenter.org*

 TV SHOW TIP

Are you a **Gossip Girl** or **Glee** fan? Some scenes were shot right there on the main square. Also across the street, you will see the **Empire Hotel** *(10 Lincoln Center Plaza)*, home to one of Gossip Girl's most famous characters: Chuck Bass.

6 In that area, you will also find a **Bed Bath & Beyond** store (1932 Broadway).

 MOVIE TIP

Are you a Ghostbusters fan? The building located at 55 Central Park West (between 65th and 66th street) served as one of the movie's settings, the Spook Central.

7 Walk on 59th Street and you'll reach **Columbus Circle**, one of my favorite places in NY. The grand statue at the center is dedicated to Christopher Columbus. Another interesting fact: The official distance from New York to any other place is measured from Columbus Circle.

8 Also, head to **The Shops at Columbus Circle**, a shopping mall in the **Time Warner Center** with several shops, restaurants, and even a *Whole Foods*. Also, good for a bathroom break! If interested, incredible and sophisticated restaurants await you on the upper floors such as *MASA, Per Se, Landmarc* and *Porter House*. On the 35th floor of the Mandarin **Oriental Hotel**, you also find **Asiate** ($$ to $$$$), with a beautiful view and delicious food.

■ Located at Freedom Place South between West 59th Street and West 61st Street, at the **Waterline Square** development you will find a public park with a nice playground for the kids and events happening throughout the year. Good spot to relax and people watch.

- For quick and healthy snacks, there is not only a Whole Foods Market but also a Fresh and Co., Juice Press and Juice Generation nearby for smoothies, salads and more, including vegan and gluten-free options.

 MOVIE TIP

Three movies that were also filmed around **Columbus Circle:** *Enchanted, Person of Interest, and Ghostbusters.*

 WINTER TIP

During the month of December, you can check out the **Holiday Market at Columbus Circle**, with several vendors selling products and snacks.

 SHOPPING

If you feel like shopping, besides The Shops At Columbus Circle there is also a *TJ Maxx* and a *Nordstrom* nearby.

WHERE TO EAT

Turnstyle - $ to $$
This underground food court located inside Columbus Circle Subway Station offers all types of food, from japanese to grilled cheese and pizza! You don't need to buy a subway ticket to access it.

Nobu Fifty Seven - $$$$
40 West 57th Street
The famous Japanese restaurant doesn't disappoint. There is another one downtown.

More options on page 83!

McGee's - $ to $$
240 West 55th Street
If you are a fan of *How I Met Your Mother*, this pub is the bar that inspired the creation of McLaren's, the show's famous pub. There are several photos of the actors hanging on the walls and the food and drinks are okay!

Robert - $$$
2 Columbus Circle
The restaurant inside the Museum of Art and Design building. Make a reservation to request a table by the window for a beautiful view of Central Park and Columbus Circle!

More options on page 83!

9 If in the mood, head to the famous **Carnegie Hall** *(881 7th Avenue)* which was completed in 1891 and is one of the world's most prestigious music halls. If you like a good show, check out the official website to see if there is anything that interests you. It is at the corner of 57th Street and 7th Avenue.

10 With the day coming to an end, I suggest catching a **Broadway** or **off Broadway show** or one of the shows at the **Jazz at Lincoln Center**, which is actually inside the Time Warner Center. Or go shopping, check out restaurants...

or just rest, because everyone needs a break!

WEDNESDAY

"I look out the window and I see
the lights and the skyline and
the people on the street rushing
around looking for action,
love, and the world's greatest
chocolate chip cookie, and my
heart does a little dance..."

Nora Ephron

The day will be filled with different places to explore, so let's start early to make the most out of it!

 To see today's free attractions, see page 119.

HOW TO GET THERE

 Take Subway **W** **R** and get off at **23rd Street** station.

SUGGESTED BREAKFAST (OR LUNCH)

• **Caffè Lavazza (Eataly)**
200 5th Avenue

• **Eisenberg**
174 Fifth Avenue, between 22nd and 23rd street

• **Maman**
22 W 25th Street

• **La Pecora Bianca**
1133 Broadway

• **Cha Cha Matcha**
1158 Broadway

• **Ralph's Coffee**
160 5th AVenue

Fishs Eddy
889 Broadway
Beautiful kitchen and home decor store.

Harry Potter Store
935 Broadway
A world of products from Harry Potter films and books. Potterhead, prepare your wand...I mean, wallet!

TJ Maxx
620 6th Avenue
Discounted department store selling clothes, accessories, home decor items and more.

Harmon Face Values
675 6th Avenue
Beauty items, makeup, travel size items, cleaning supplies, personal hygiene products for a reasonable price and much more!

Michael's
675 6th Avenue
Art and craft store that also sells DIY items for parties, weddings, special occasions, stationery, photo frames, scrapbooking, etc.

Pottery Barn
12 W 20th Street
Home decor, furniture and more.

Other cool stores to check out in the area: Adorama (electronics), **Burlington** and **Marshalls** (similar to TJ Maxx), **The Container Store** (organization items for home / office), **Trader Joe's** (budget friendly supermarket), **Buy Buy Baby** (everything for babies and items for pregnant women), **CAMP** (a fun toy store for kids! They offer craft classes as well, make sure you ask to see the magic door), **Kleinfeld and David's Bridal** (bridal dress stores).

FLATIRON BUILDING

Built in 1902, this 22- story building, originally called the **Fuller Building**, was one of the city's first skyscrapers. Located at the intersection of 5th Avenue and Broadway between 22nd and 23rd street. It got the name Flatiron because It resembles a flat iron! Across from it you will find **Madison Square Park**, great for people watching, a picnic and if you have kids, the playground is fun. The park offers various activities in the summer. There is a **Shake Shack** here and **Eataly** is right across the street!

Take the subway **W** **R** OR walk (I highly recommend walking) towards downtown and get off at 14th Street, where **Union Square Park** is located, another place that has stolen my heart since day one!
If you pay attention, you will see an impressive 1856 statue of George Washington. The square attracts all people and tribes and is surrounded by shops, banks, hotels, theaters and even a green market! **TIP:** Go to **Burlington** for a beautiful aeriel view of Union Square!

TIP

If you like the show Friends, be sure to visit **THE FRIENDS Experience**! *130 E 23rd Street*. Tickets and more information: www.friendstheexperience.com

💡 SUGGESTION

Some other shops to check out nearby:

If you like comics, superheroes, toy art and animation in general, be sure to stop by **Forbidden Planet** *(832 Broadway)*.

And for sneaker lovers, from the most common to the most exclusive, **Flight Club** *(812 Broadway)* is a must!

The **Strand Bookstore** is a huge independent bookstore. You will also find stationery and Souvenirs and bargain books! Despite the close proximity to the giant **Barnes and Noble** *(828 Broadway)*, it is the most popular in the area.

Barnes and Noble Bookstore is another favorite of mine. It is a good place to refuel at the cafe with a Starbucks coffee, grab a pastry, sandwich or enjoy a light snack.

At Union Square's famous **Greenmarket** you'll find a little bit of everything: bread, flowers, fruit, vegetables and other organic produce from small farmers. It happens every Monday, Wednesday, Friday and Saturday from 8 am to 6 pm.

In November (and December), there is a nice **Holiday Market** with little shops selling treats and different kinds of products from winter accessories to candles and handmade jewelry.

Murray's Bagels - $
500 6th Avenue
Don't leave New York without trying a traditional toasted bagel with cream cheese! Or make your own bagel sandwich!

Max Brenner - $$
841 Broadway
If you like chocolate, this is the place to be. The food is also good.

Basta Pasta - $$
37 West 17th Street
Where Japanese and Italian cuisines blend gracefully! The famous spaghetti mixed inside a huge slab of Parmesan cheese was popular on social media. If possible, make a reservation!

Paddy Maguire's Ale House - $ a $$
237 3rd Avenue
An Irish tavern with pool tables, TV screens displaying sports games and drinks for a fair price.

IHOP - $$
235 E 14th St
Pancakes, waffles and traditional American dinner food.

Peacefood Café - $ to $$
41 East 11th Street
A vegan café and restaurant serving sandwiches, pasta, salads, pastries and much more!

Raclette - $$
511 E 12th St
For cheese lovers, this is your place!

3 From there you can walk OR take the subway **W** **R** **towards downtown** to Prince Street OR the subway **6** to **Spring Street.**

4 You'll arrive in the heart of SoHo, a neighborhood with incredible architecture and fashion!

First, you should know that there are specific geographic denomination for this area, but let's simplify to make it easier:

SoHo → South of Houston Street (neighborhood south of Houston Street)

NoHo → North of Houston Street (neighborhood north of Houston Street)

Nolita → North of Little Italy (neighborhood north of Little Italy)

I didn't write a specific SoHo itinerary for you to follow, the best part of SoHo is walking around... Not sure where to start? Here are three of my favorite streets: **Prince Street, Mulberry** and **Spring Street**.

TIP
If you like rooftop bars and want to have a beautiful view of the area, **Last Light** is a rooftop located on the eleventh floor of the Sister City hotel and has a nice open space to enjoy the day with good drinks and snacks! *225 Bowery*

And of course Broadway, where you will find popular stores like *Converse, H&M, Zara, Uniqlo, Sephora, lululemon, Footlocker and Bloomingdale's, etc...*

WHERE TO EAT (SOHO | NOHO | NOLITA)

Tacombi - $$
67 Elizabeth St
Authentic Mexican food in a
casual atmosphere.

Jack's wife Freda - $$
224 Lafayette St
American-Mediterranean food
and cocktails.

The Butcher's daughter - $$
581 Hudson St
Beautiful vegetarian restaurant.

Pietro Nolita - $$
174 Elizabeth Street
Italian food in a cozy and pink atmosphere.

Little Prince - $$ to $$$
199 Prince Street
Cute french bistro.

Il Buco - $$ to $$$
47 Bond Street
Upscale Mediterranean-Italian with a
beautiful wine cellar in the basement.

Black Tap - $$
529 Broome Street
Creative hamburgers and milkshakes.

Balthazar - $$$
80 Spring Street
Elegant but casual French restaurant.

Freemans - $$$
Freeman Alley
This hidden-away spot serves American fare,
craft cocktails and more!

Bar Pitti - $$
268 6th Ave
Italian restaurant - also a popular place
among celebrities.

Cipriani - $$$ to $$$$
376 West Broadway
An upscale Italian restaurant.

SoHo Park - $ to $$
62 Prince Street
Salads and sandwiches in a casual setting

**Last light rooftop (on the 11th floor of the
Sister City hotel)**
62 Prince Street
Salads and sandwiches in a casual setting.

UNDER $10

Don't leave SoHo without trying at least one of these:

- **Dominique Ansel Bakery's** *($ - 189 Spring Street)* sweets and famous cronuts
- French macarons, desserts from **Ladurée** ($ to $$$ - *398 W Broadway*)
- The famous grilled corn from **Café Habana** ($ to $$ - *17 Prince Street*)
- **Prince Street Pizza** Slice *($ - 27 Prince Street)*
- Try one of the many Rice pudding flavors at **Rice to Riches** *($ - 37 Spring St)*

MY FAVORITE SHOPS IN SOHO

Bag All
219 Mott St
Bags for pretty much everything you need when traveling and organizing.

Olfactory
281 Mott St
You can customize your own perfume scent and bottle.

Artists and Fleas
490 Broadway
A space that brings together fashion sellers/artists, crafts and vintage things.

Housing Works Bookstore Cafe & Bar
126 Crosby Street
Used books, CDs, DVDs, comic books and a nice cafe in the back. There is also a Housing Works Thrift Shop next to it.

Bite Beauty Lab
174 Prince Street | www.bitebeauty.com/lip-labs/lip-lab-nyc
Make an appointment to create your own lipstick.

Paper Source
83 Spring Street
One of my favorite NY stationery stores. There are other locations around the city as well.

Amazon 4 Star
72 Spring St
A nice selection with products rated 4 stars and up on Amazon.

TIP
There are great streetwear-style boutiques:
Supreme: 190 Bowery
BAPE Store: 91 Greene Street
Carhartt Work in Progress: 119 Crosby Street

5 The beautiful **Greene Street** is one of my favorites, the architecture is amazing and you will find shops like *Louis Vuitton, Balenciaga, Stella McCartney, Dior*, among many others.

◾ If you have time, I recommend a quick stop by **NoMo Soho Hotel**. The entrance became a popular location on Instagram and the **Nomo Kitchen Restaurant** serves lunch, dinner, breakfast and nice drinks. (*$$$ - 9 Crosby Street*).

PLACES TO VISIT in SOHO and its surroundings

Earth Room *(141 Wooster Street | www.diaart.org)*
Created by the artist Walter de Maria, it is a unique sculpture that has been there since 1977 and contains more than 300m and 127,000 kilos of land. Entrance is free.

Ghost Building *(102 Prince Street)*
The iconic building that was used in the movie Ghost.

Apple Store *(103 Prince Street)*
Usually less busy than the other ones in Midtown.

New York City Fire Museum *(278 Spring Street | www.nycfiremuseum.org)*
Fun option for those who are traveling with children.

Elizabeth Street Garden
The garden is open to the public between Prince and Spring Street. It is quite simple but very important to the people that preserve it with the help of volunteers and donations.

New Museum
The New Museum of Contemporary Art is a beautiful museum founded in 1977. Admission price is U$18 per adult but on Thursday evenings from 7 p.m.–9 p.m. you can Pay-What-You-Wish. Suggested Minimum: U$2

If you are not sure how to get to the heart of Little Italy simply put **Italian American Museum** on your GPS. If you want to know more about the history of Italians in the USA, I recommend visiting it. They also have permanent and temporary exhibitions. *155 Mulberry Street | italianamericanmuseum.org*

7 This is what locals call the most touristy version of the Italian colony in NY claiming the Little Italy in the Bronx to be the most authentic (more on that later!) But I have eaten in many restaurants around this neighborhood and I have had good experiences in general. At lunchtime most restaurants offer lunch specials, you can have a good meal for about $15 per person (plus tips and fees).

🔔 WHERE TO EAT (LITTLE ITALY)

La Mela - $$
167 Mulberry Street
Traditional Italian food with a casual atmosphere.

Caffe Palermo - $
148 Mulberry Street
For cannolis and other delights.

Lombardi's - $$
32 Spring Street
NY's oldest pizzeria. They have been serving the traditional thin Neapolitan pizza since 1905.

Café Napoli - $ to $$
191 Hester Street
Traditional restaurant in the area for coffee, pastries and sweets.

6

If you follow **Mulberry Street** where the main restaurants are, you will hit Canal Street in **Chinatown**. You will start noticing Chinese signs along the way and eventually the vibe changes and hey, you're in China in the middle of NYC! Yes, as the name implies, it's a taste of China in NY. And you can find everything here: great restaurants, souvenirs, beauty stores, Chinese products, and designer replicas of various brands, cafes, hotels and many restaurants.

TIP
On *www.freetoursbyfoot.com* you can choose from a number of free NY walking tours, including some exclusive to Chinatown, SoHo, and Little Italy. Pay as much as you wish.

Canal, *Pell* and *Doyers Street* are some of the most famous streets! But there are many interesting places to see in the area ... I have selected some of the most popular for you!

- **Mahayana Buddhist Temple:** *133 Canal Street*. Opened in 1997, it is the largest Buddhist temple in NY, with the largest statue of Buddha.

- It is worth checking out the entrance to the **Manhattan Bridge**, designed by the same architects who created the New York Public Library.

- **Pell Street e Doyers Street:** curved and filled with colors and signs, flags and old buildings. To get into the mood, there are two popular restaurants in this area: **Joe's Shangai** ($$ - 9 Pell Street), specializing in dumplings! And the **Nom Wah Tea Parlor** ($$ - 13 Doyers Street) with the famous dim sum and Chinese dumplings. Usually, you will see people lining up especially on nights and weekends.

- **Kimlau Memorial Arch**: Located at *Kimlau Square*, created by Americans and offered to Chinese Americans who died in World War II fighting for democracy. It is named in honor of Benjamin Ralph Kimlau, a Chinese-American who lost his life during a mission in 1944, when his plane crashed.

- **Church of the Transfiguration:** *29 Mott Street.* The largest Chinese Catholic church in the Western world. Masses in English, Mandarin, and Cantonese!

- If you like video games and arcade vibes, there are some options in Chinatown, like the **Chinatown Fair Video Games** *(8 Mott St).*

NIGHTLIFE

Apotheke - $$ to $$$$
9 Doyers Street
At night, this is the right destination to have good cocktails, enjoy live music and jazz!

TIP

For those wishing to dive into the history of the area check the **Museum of Chinese in America**: *215 Centre Street - mocanyc.org*

EAT | CHINATOWN

Jing Fong - $$
20 Elizabeth St
Super traditional in the area, there may be a line to enter.

Xi'an Famous Foods - $
67 Bayard Street
With other locations in NY, this is a popular modern chinese restaurant chain.

Joe's Shangai - $$
9 Pell Street
Specializing in dumplings!

Nom Wah Tea Parlor - $$
13 Doyers Street
Famous dim sum and Chinese dumplings.

Vanessa's Dumpling House - $
118 Eldridge Street
Cheap fried or steamed dumplings, buns, noodles and more.

Buddha Bodai Kosher Vegetarian Restaurant - $ to $$
5 Mott Street
A Chinese vegan restaurant. My favorite in the area.

🍺 LEAVING CHINATOWN

If you still have energy, I recommend ending the day on the **Lower East Side.**
You can get there by walking, uber/taxi or using Google Maps to see which
subway line is the closest to the desired location. I recommend the lines F, J,
M or Z:

Live music fan? Here are some suggestions to enjoy live music with a young and
local vibe:
Pianos *(158 Ludlow Street)*
Arlene's Grocery *(95 Stanton Street)*

🍽 WHERE TO EAT

Dirty French - $$$
180 Ludlow Street
One of the coolest and trendiest
restaurants in the city bringing
traditional French cuisine with
influences from various parts of
the world. They serve breakfast,
lunch, brunch, and dinner.

Sons of Essex - $$$
133 Essex St New York
Bar and restaurant with vintage
decor. American food and drinks
with a lot of music and DJ.

Mr Purple - $$$
180 Orchard Street
Rooftop bar on the fifteenth floor
of Hotel Indigo.

Souvlaki Greek - $ to $$
116 Stanton Street
The decor of the place takes you to Mykonos
and the typical Greek food is quite tasty!

Beauty & Essex - $$$
146 Essex Street
A speakeasy bar: from the outside, an
ordinary pawn store. But a door inside gives
access to one of the hottest restaurants in the
downtown area, recreating the prohibition
era feel when drinking alcohol was illegal
so secret places were arranged for those
interested.

Essex Market
88 Essex Street
Different eateries with something for everyone

TIP

If you love cats, there is a cat cafe in the area! You can play or simply watch them interact with other customers. There is a fee per person (U$20 in 2020). Check the website for updated prices and hours!
(26 Clinton St. | www.konekonyc.com)

The **New york Botanical garden** (*2900 Southern Blvd | www.nybg.org*) in the Bronx has free admission every Wednesday for NYC residents.

Jazz at St. Peter's Church (*619 Lexington Avenue | www.saintpeters.org/jazz/*)offers a jazz show every Wednesday from 1pm-2pm. They ask for a donation, the suggested price is U$10.

New York Aquarium (*602 Surf Ave | nyaquarium.com*) offers a pay what you wish admission on Wednesdays at 3pm.

The Bronx Zoo (*2300 Southern Blvd | bronxzoo.com*) is the largest metropolitan zoo in the world and on Wednesdays you pay as much as you wish to get in.

Staten Island Zoo (*614 Broadway | www.statenislandzoo.org*) aquarium, birds and more. Free entrance on Wednesdays after 2 pm.

> *"Everybody ought to have a Lower East Side in their life."*
>
> **Irving Berlin**

THURSDAY

Downtown is one of NY's greatest historical treasures and the architecture is simply beautiful. Ready to explore and go back in time?

 To see today's free attractions, see page 133.

HOW TO GET THERE

Subway lines **1** *South Ferry*, **4** **5** *Bowling Green* OR **W** **R** *Whitehall Street / South Ferry.*

SUGGESTED BREAKFAST

• **Starbucks**
One Battery Park Plaza

• **Le Pain Quotidien**
85 Broad Street

• **Leo's Bagels**
3 Hanover Square

• **Dunkin' Donuts**
33 Beaver Street

STATUE OF LIBERTY

Ok, once in New York, I truly recommend not missing the chance to see the Statue of Liberty either up close or from afar. And if you are taking the official ferry to Liberty Island, to make the journey as pleasant as possible, arrive early (I'd be the first in line if possible) because lines can get really long later on the day. There is a security check before you board the ferry.

1 Hours of operation vary according to the season, but in general the first ferry leaves at 8:30 and 9:30 am in the winter (January to March). Tickets cost about $20 per adult, depending on where you buy it. To go up to the statue's crown or pedestal, purchase your ticket online beforehand on the official website www.statuecruises.com

 Caution: Don't buy your ticket from street vendors, use only the official ticket office near the boarding area.

■ If you don't want to do this paid tour, take the **Staten Island Ferry** (for free) to see the statue from a distance and a wonderful Manhattan view! To get to the station from where the ferry departs, take any of the subway lines mentioned earlier. Each ride takes about 25 minutes.

■ If you want to explore the Staten Island area, you can easily spend a day: You will find museums, an aquarium, a zoo, a fort, beach, a Primark and the Empire Outlets.

2 Once you're back from the Statue of Liberty tour or Staten Island Ferry, walk (about 5-10 minutes) to **Fraunces Tavern Restaurant** *($$$ - 54 Pearl Street)*. It opens at 11 in the morning. The place is not just another restaurant in NY. The original building was built in 1719, it was rebuilt and yet it is one of the oldest in the city. Several political meetings with George Washington (the first US President) took place there during the American Revolution. It serves brunch, lunch, and dinner, and has more than 200 whiskeys and 130 types of beer and other drinks. On the second floor there is a museum ($7 per adult). *www.frauncestavern.com*

3 From there, head for two of my favorite streets in the city: Pearl Street and Stone Street, a cobblestone street that claims to be the first paved street in NY... a real treasure! Restored impeccably, there are bars and restaurants on both sides. In the summer, the tables outside are an invitation to get to know what New York's happy hour has to offer! Hungry? You will find pizza, burgers, pasta, Mexican food, beer, sweets and more! **There are so many good restaurant and bar options but I will list some suggestions below:**

🍽 WHERE TO EAT

Mad Dog & Beans - $$
83 Pearl Street (there is also an entrance on Stone Street)
I love this place for Mexican and Latin food.

Bavaria Bierhaus - $$
19 S William Street (there is also an entrance on Stone Street)
German bar and restaurant. They serve brunch, lunch, dinner and a good variety of beers and drinks.

The Cauldron New York - $$
47 Stone Street
Wizard-themed for a real potions experience and good food

Ulysses' A Folk House - $$
95 Pearl Street
Charming pub and typical Irish restaurant, I love the vibe!

Adriennes Pizza Bar - $ to $$
54 Stone Street
Pizza, salads, pasta, sandwiches, beers, and wines.

▮ OTHER PLACES OF INTEREST IN THE AREA

New York Vietnam Veterans Memorial Plaza; Hanover Square; The Queen Elizabeth II; September 11th Garden; Skyscraper Museum.

If you wish to take the NYC Ferry to other parts of NYC, there is a ferry terminal nearby (**Wall Street Terminal**).

4 From there head to **Seaport District** *(19 Fulton Street)* where Pier 17 is located - harshly hit by Hurricane Sandy a few years ago. Much has changed and different shops and restaurants have opened. You will see beautiful views of the Brooklyn Bridge and the East River. In the winter, the **Winterland Rink**, an ice skating rink is installed on the *Rooftop of Pier 17.*

WHAT ELSE TO DO THERE?

In addition to dining and shopping in the area you can also learn more about the history of NYC:

- The **Southstreet Seaport Museum** is a collection of different buildings and things you can see and experience, such as galleries, sail boats and even a printing company. Most of them are paid but are included in some attraction passes.

- **Bowne and Co Stationers** *(211 Water St)*
  Established in 1775, this unique stationery store is the oldest in the city and keeps the history of the region alive by printing customized work using old methods as the iconics 19th-century machines! You will find stationery items such as notebooks, some books, cards, some souvenirs. Free entrance.

- Next to it you will find **Bowne Printers**, which also offers printing services and they use the historic machines from the museum to this day. They can only accept small batches of orders and they offer workshops as well.

Other places to see:

- Traveling with kids? The **Imagination Playground** on John Street between South Street and Front Street is a great option for the kids! Just put the name on your GPS.

WHERE TO EAT IN THE AREA

Front Street and its surroundings is a great place to eat, explore as you wish but here are some suggestions:

Pier 17 - $$ to $$$$
89 South Street
Renowned shops and restaurants with beautiful views of the Brooklyn Bridge. The R17 restaurant is one of my favorites and in the warmer months, you can sit outside and enjoy the view of downtown Manhattan.

Jeremy's Ale House - $
228 Front Street
Adorned with bras hanging from the ceiling, this place has been a classic spot for over 40 years, they serve seafood, American food, and huge beers.

By Chloe - $ to $$
181 Front Street
A vegan restaurant that serves breakfast, lunch, snacks, sandwiches, salads, and desserts.

Cafe Patoro - $
223 Front Street
A Brazilian coffee shop serving traditional pão de queijo (cheese bread) and much more

- If you want to buy discount Broadway tickets but don't want to wait in the long lines you find in Times Square, there is a TKTS office right here: *190 Front Street.*

- **IPIC Theater** *(11 Fulton Street)*
  Recline your seat and enjoy a meal while watching a movie!

- **Titanic Memorial Park**
  You will probably notice the 60-foot-tall (18 m) lighthouse at the corner of Pearl and Fulton Street. It was built to honor the people who died on the RMD Titanic on April 15, 1912.

TIP

Federal Reserve Bank Museum and Gold Vault Tour
This experience is very popular and you need to make a reservation 30 days in advance. On the tour you learn about the responsibilities of the Federal Reserve Bank and you can see a gold vault! Visit the official website to book: *www.newyorkfed. org/aboutthefed/visiting*

5 Now, let's head to Wall Street and take a photo with the famous **Wall Street Charging Bull** (*corner of Broadway and Morris Street*). This area is full of history and things to explore, such as the **Federal Hall Building** (*26 Wall Street*), a place that has had many functions, among them the place of George Washington's first speech, the first National Congress and Supreme Court, among other important milestones. Today it operates as a free museum and a memorial to the first president of the United States and the history of the country.

6 From Wall Street, walk to **Trinity Church** (*75 Broadway*) and **St. Paul's Chapel** (*209 Broadway*), which survived the attacks on September 11, 2001. Inside, you will find a small memorial with history, photos and objects that mark the attacks.

7 From there I suggest a stop at **The Oculus** and its interior, the **Westfield World Trade Center**, a shopping mall inside the station that connects subways from NYC to the PATH train, train lines going to New Jersey. Santiago Calatrava's architecture was created to emulate a dove in flight. If you stand in the middle of the main lobby, when you look up you can see the beautiful Freedom Tower.

8 From there, head to the **9/11 Memorial** (*180 Greenwich Street*), where you will find the two memorial pools built where the two twin towers were destroyed in the attack of September 11. The memorial is free. Also, you can stop by the Survivor Tree, a callery pear tree that survived the attacks, it's located close to one of the pools.

9 If you're interested in visiting the **9/11 Museum**, allocate at least an hour to it. Tickets cost (in 2019): $24 adult, $18 seniors (+65), $18 student and $15 from 7-17 years old. The museum offers free access every Tuesday from 5 pm | *www.911memorial.org/museum*, you can try to reserve tickets two weeks before the desired Tuesday or head to the museum around 4pm for a first come first serve tickets.

👤 DID YOU KNOW?

• When visiting the 9/11 Memorial, you will probably find white roses placed on names of some of the victims. These roses are placed daily indicating that that day would have been their birthday.

• Close to the Memorial, you can also find some monitors, where you can search, find and know more about the victim's history. It's another way to **NEVER FORGET.**

10 Now, if you are up for it, we will walk to one of the beautiful observatories in New York: the **One World Observatory.** The general admission price is $ 35 (2020). I recommend buying tickets in advance to avoid lines. To purchase your ticket, visit the official website. It is also included in the Sightseeing Pass. Allocate about 1- 2 hours for the experience.

11 From here head to Brookfield Place (230 Vesey Street), an upscale shopping mall with nice stores, a gorgeous Hudson River view, the famous Le District, an incredible French market with restaurants and everything else you can imagine and a beautiful food hall on the second floor. The view of the Hudson River is my favorite thing about it.

■ And it is also next to one of my favorite parks: Battery Park City. Great place to rest a bit and enjoy the view at sunset. If you are traveling with kids, this is a good place with playgrounds to go!
   » Oh! There's a **Shake Shack** (*215 Murray Street*) over there too!

TIP

If you are in the warmer months and are in the mood for a relaxing evening, you can end the day here and walk along the Hudson River Greenway (Hudson River Park) until you reach Pier 26. I love seeing the sunset from there! And right next to it, on **Pier 25** you will find a beach volleyball court, a mini golf, a playground and you can even go kayaking for free! Great option for families. And for a casual but nice dinner, **City Vineyard** is one of my favorite restaurants in the area!

 MOVIE TIP

If you are a **Ghostbusters** fan, visit the Firehouse, Hook & Ladder Company 8 located at *14 North Moore Street and Varick Street.*

■ **COOL SHOPS IN THE REGION**
   The Mysterious Bookshop
   58 Warren Street
   A bookstore specializing in fiction, suspense, crime, and espionage books.

 PHOTO OP

If you enjoy different backgrounds for photos, **Staple Street** is one of the most unique and instagrammable spots in the area.

🍽 WHERE TO EAT

Brookfield Place - Le District - $ to $$$
225 Liberty Street
A food hall serving French delights.

Stage Door Delicatessen - $
26 Vesey Street
A deli that serves a nice variety of pizzas and was in the movie The Godfather.

The ODEON- $$
145 W Broadway
A bistro opened in the 1980s and that is still one of the locals' favorites.

12 ## NOW, IF YOU STILL HAVE ENERGY, LET'S EXPLORE A LITTLE MORE OF THE LOWER EAST SIDE

Take the subway **R** **W** (Station 8 Street - NYU) or **6** (Astor Place) heading **Uptown**.

■ To end the night in a fun mood, I recommend two famous Indian restaurants **Panna II** (93 1st Avenue) or **Milon** (same address). Good, relatively cheap and tasty, and with very colorful decor. They only accept payment in cash and don't sell alcoholic beverages. If it's your birthday they will offer you free ice cream and sing happy birthday. Don't expect great service but it is part of the experience.

■ For a unique experience check out **Please Don't Tell** *($-$$$ - 113 St. Marks Place)*, a speakeasy bar that has its entrance through a phone booth inside a hot dog shop. An interesting experience for sure! Make reservations or at least grab a hot dog at Crif Dogs.

■ Not sure where to go? Head to **St. Marks Place**, a fun street with many Japanese restaurants, shops, karaoke bars, tattoo parlors, and small shops between 3rd and Avenue A. I really enjoy walking around at night!

🍽 WHERE TO EAT

Spot Dessert Bar - $ to $$
13 St. Marks Place
A bar serving creative and delicious desserts!

Ramen Setagaya - $$
34 ½ St. Marks Place
The famous Japanese noodles!

Decibel Sake bar - $$
240 East 9th Street
Cool underground sake bar!

Cha-An - $$
230 East 9th Street
A restaurant specializing in Japanese desserts but also serving traditional dishes. The decoration resembles a Japanese tea house!

VSPOT - $ to $$
12 St. Marks Place
Latin vegan food.

Odd Fellows Ice Cream - $
75 East 4th Street
Super yummy ice creams!

Veselka - $ to $$
144 2nd Avenue
Ukrainian Restaurant! The pierogis are super famous!

Risotteria Melotti - $$
309 E 5th St
Specialized in risottos - vegetarian options available.

Ladybird - $$
111 E 7th St
Vegetarian/vegan restaurant and bar with creative drinks.

McSorley's Old Ale House - $
15 East 7th Street
An old bar/pub, bizarre decor, and a totally casual atmosphere.

Crocodile Lounge - $
325 east 14th street
Get a mini pizza with every drink you order!

▶ MOVIE TIP

An iconic scene from the movie **When Harry Met Sally** was shot at **Katz's Delicatessen** *($$ - 205 East Houston Street)*, home to the famous pastrami sandwich.

◼ COOL SHOPS

Pink Olive | *439 E 9th Street*
Stationery with a variety of gifts and decorative items.

Videogames New York | *202 E 6th Street*
A store specializing in video games including rare games.

Mr. Throwback | *437 E 9th Street*
Nostalgic items from the 90s, like sneakers, t-shirts, toys, etc.

Toy Tokyo | *91 2nd Avenue*
A shop dedicated to collectible toys in general, including anime, comics, and games.

Casey Rubber Stamps | *322 E 11th Street*
A small shop where you can buy or create your own stamp.

The **Tenement Museum** *(103 Orchard St | www.tenement.org)* is an interesting opportunity to learn the development of NY and the region that once was one of the most populous in the world! There are different guided tours available, including touring the apartments that were once home to more than 15,000 people from more than 20 countries between 1863 and 2011 - and it operates as a museum today. Each tour costs $25 per adult (2019).

The **New Museum** *(235 Bowery Street | www.newmuseum.org)* is a contemporary art museum with several exhibitions in an interesting architectural building. It costs $18 per adult (2020). On Thursdays between 7pm and 9pm, you pay what you wish, the minimum price suggested is $2. Check out the website for more information.

The **Essex Market** *(88 Essex Street)* is a modern market perfect for snacks, drinks and even grocery shopping.

The **Tompkins Square Park** is a nice park to rest, observe the local life or have a picnic. Many food options in this area.

Joe's Pub & The Public Theater *(425 Lafayette Street | www.publictheater.org)* If you want something more cultural and with a more local atmosphere, be sure to check the website for shows and events of these two iconic spots in the area.

International Center of Photography Museum (ICP) *(79 Essex Street)* If you enjoy photography like me (if you missed the introduction of the book, I'm a photographer here in New York - @fotografaemnovayork) ICP is an interesting option! There are exhibitions, history, programs and workshops throughout the year. Website: *www.icp.org*.

 The Whitney Museum of American Art offers Pay What You Wish on Thursdays, 1:30–6 pm. Advance ticketing required.

> *"I regret profoundly that I was not an American and not born in Greenwich Village. It might be dying, and there might be a lot of dirt in the air you breathe, but this is where it's happening".*
>
> **John Lennon**

FRIDAY

TIP

Check out the restaurants to end the night in the *Meatpacking District*. Make reservations if needed.

 See **page 145** for the free attractions.

 HOW TO GET THERE

 Take Subway **1** and get off at **Christopher Street/Sheridan Square**.

SUGGESTED BREAKFAST

• **Buvette**
42 Grove Street

• **Magnolia Bakery**
We will get there in a minute.

• **Starbucks**
Next to the station

① GREENWHICH VILLAGE

Let's start the day at the beautifull *Greenwich Village*, scene of several movies and TV series such as *Friends, Sex and The City, Spider-Man* and many others. After you get off the station, walk through Grove Street until you reach the address: 90 Bedford Street. This is where you will find the apartment from the show **FRIENDS** *(90 Bedford Street)*. Even if you are not a fan it is worth the picture, so you can send it to your friends who love the series, like me! I'd love to see your photos, tag me on instagram **@marthasachser**

OTHER POINTS OF INTEREST AROUND:

- *Grove Court*: Six townhouses that were completed between 1853 and 1854 with a private square on one of the most beautiful streets of Greenwich Village.

- *Cherry Lane Theater*: Theater opened in 1924. *38 Commerce Street*

- *75 1/2 Bedford Street*, the narrowest house in NY, some artists have lived in it and despite its size, it's worth a lot of money!

- *Saint Luke's Place*, a charming street in the area with 15 houses from the 1850s. The exterior of house number 10 was used in the series *The Cosby Show (10 Leroy Street)* and the movie *Wait Until Dark* with Audrey Hepburn.

② Head to **Magnolia Bakery** *(401 Bleecker Street)*. Walking through the streets of NY always grants great surprises. Take a picture with one of the famous cupcakes or recreat the scene of the show Sex and the City. And since you are there, go to 66 Perry Street, this is the house used as Carrie Bradshaw's apartment.

③ Then head to *Bleecker Street*, one of my favorites! I recommend choosing a place to eat and recharge there if you haven't eaten anything yet.

🕵️ DID YOU KNOW?

The Stonewall Inn was the site of the Stonewall Riots in 1969. This protest gave rise to the LGBTQ movement. Across the street you will find Christopher Park, where you can see the George Segal's Gay Liberation Monument, two same sex couples statues in honor of the gay rights movement.

🍽️ WHERE TO EAT

Joe's Pizza - $
7 Carmine Street
The pizza place from the 1st Spider-Man movie. Good and cheap pizza.

Tacombi - $
255 Bleecker St
Mexican restaurant.

Trattoria Pesce Pasta - $ to $$
262 Bleecker Street
Pasta and seafood!

Bleecker Street Pizza - $
69 7th Ave South
Voted one of the best pizza places in NY.

Palma - $$
28 Cornelia Street
Italian food with a winter garden. I highly recommend having dinner here!

By Chloe - $
185 Bleecker Street
Popular vegan fast food.

Sant Ambroeus West Village - $$
259 West 4th Street
Italian restaurant.

Olio e Piú - $$
3 Greenwich Ave
A beautiful trattoria serving thin-crust pizza and Italian wines.

🎵 LIVE MUSIC

For jazz, blues or live rock: Fat Cat (75 Christopher Street), Blue Note (131 West 3rd Street), Village Vanguard (178 7th Avenue), Wha Café (115 Macdougal Street), Arthur's Tavern (57 Grove St) and The Bitter End (147 Bleecker Street). NY's oldest rock club where Lady Gaga, Steve Wonder, Bob Dylan, Norah Jones, and many others have performed.

4 IF ARE NOT HUNGRY YET...

Head to the famous **Washington Square Park**, the backyard for New York University students and one of my favorite places! The atmosphere is nice especially between spring and fall. The arch, built in 1889 to celebrate George Washington's centennial as president, is a must-see! It also marks the beginning of 5th Avenue!

5

Head to **Macdougal Street**, a young and vibrant street in the area. I recommend passing by again at night or on the weekend when it gets busier. You will find several bars, cheap food, restaurants, comedy clubs and live music.

🍽 WHERE TO EAT

Caffe Reggio - $
119 Macdougal Street
Home of the original cappuccino since 1927. Super cozy, it has been featured in several movies like The Godfather Part 2, Shaft, among others.

Insomnia Cookies - $
116 Macdougal Street
If you like cookies, try at least the chocolate chip one. Or take it to go!

Artichoke pizza - $
111 Macdougal Street
The famous NY artichoke pizza! They offer other pizza toppings as well!

Mamoun's Falafel - $
119 MacDougal Street
If you are a falafel person like me, you can get an inexpensive falafel wrap for less than U$5.

1 street, 3 stores!

Here are some of my favorite stores in this area:

- *The Uncommons (230 Thompson St)*: If you love board games, this is the perfect place! The Uncommons is the first board game cafe in Manhattan, which means not only can you grab a coffee and get snacks, but you can also play one of many, many, many board games! They charge a fee per person if you want to play (U$10 in 2020)! Visit their website for prices and more information.

- *Generation Records (210 Thompson St)*: CDs, vinyl, posters, tees, DVDS and more! If you love music, check it out!

- *Chess Forum (219 Thompson St):* All things chess. You can play, learn and even buy unique pieces!

OK, part of the following steps of our day can also be done on a different day, perhaps if you'd like you can take the day to visit the **Hudson Yards Complex** and end with a trip to **High Line Park**. But if you have energy, here is my suggestion:

6 Take subway C or E on West 4th Street and head uptown! Get off at 23rd Street station, which is one of the busiest streets in Chelsea.

   » 23rd Street

- If you're hungry, check out the **Trailer Park Lounge** *(271 West 23rd Street)* it is a cool and relaxed restaurant/bar with peculiar decor. At night, it becomes even more fun! Another place for treats around there is the famous **Doughnut Plant** *(220 West 23rd Street)*.

7 From the station, follow 23rd Street to 10th Avenue and go up to the High Line Park (with entrances also along 14th, 16th, 18th, 20th, 23rd, 26th, 28th, 30th and 34th streets). Some of them have lift access.

8 Leave the park at 16th Street because it's time to visit the famous **Chelsea Market** *(75 9th Avenue)*, a food hall with great food options like **The Lobster Place** and several shops. It is also home to some TV shows and *YouTube Space*. **Buddakan** restaurant, very famous among *Sex and The City* fans, is right next door.

The **Whitney Museum of American Art** *(99 Gansevoort Street | whitney.org)* is nearby as well. On Fridays from 7 pm to 10 pm, the price is suggested; you pay as you wish.

If you like coffee, in 2018 a **Starbucks Reserve Roastery** *(61 9th Avenue)* was introduced. It's an incredible space dedicated to a selection of the best coffee beans, you can also have coffee inspired cocktails, have a coffee tasting or order delicious pastries or savory snacks.

Ground Zero Museum Workshop *(420 W 14th St 2)* is a small interactive museum dedicated to educating visitors about 9/11 so children are welcome. The museum accepts the New York Pass and the New York Explorer Pass. If you haven't gotten the pass, admission costs $25 per adult (in 2019) and it is closed on Mondays and Tuesdays.

8 From there, we'll explore the *Meatpacking District*. One of the coolest neighborhoods in the city, with great dining, nightlife, art galleries and even a gourmet market, the **Gansevoort Market** *(353 West 14th Street)*.
There's always some cool event or some exhibition going on in the area and despite the fresh vibe, the cobblestone streets add a special touch to the neighborhood bringing us back to the past. If you want to see what is happening right now, the neighborhood keeps their official website updated with the latest news, events and even restaurants you can check out: *www. meatpacking-district.com*

9 If you are not in the mood for nightlife, I highly recommend ending the day watching the sun set on **Little Island**, this beautiful floating island on *Pier 55, in Hudson River Park, at 14th Street* (scheduled to open in late spring 2021).

💡 DID YOU KNOW?

Back in the day, the neighborhood was originally a residential one with some markets here and there but it became a commercial area when in 1900 a large number of meat houses operated there.

 WHERE TO EAT

Catch - $$$
21 9th Avenue
One of the trendiest restaurants in town, young vibe, fun, and good food. They have a rooftop too. Make a reservation!

Fig & Olive - $$ to $$$
420 West 13th Street
Butter-free. Here the main ingredient is olive oil, seasonings, and flavors from the south of France, Italy, and Spain.

The Frying Pan - $$
Big Red Boat in Park, 207 12th Ave
How about dinner on a boat with lots of drinks and tasty appetizers? It's open from May until October - weather permitting.

TAO - $$$
92 9th Ave
It has a beautiful interior and an Asian fusion menu in a sophisticated atmosphere.

Santina - $$$
820 Washington Street
Italian fresh food. Modern vibe and seafood.

The Standard Grill - $$
848 Washington Street
Serving breakfast, lunch, brunch, and dinner.

Plunge - $$$
Rooftop bar at the Hotel Gansevoort.

NIGHTLIFE IN THE AREA

Beergarden | Standard Hotel - $$
848 Washington Street
A brewery with an Oktoberfest vibe and a young atmosphere.

Le Bain and The Top of The Standard - $$ to $$$
848 Washington Street
The famous rooftop bar at the top of the Standard Hotel offers drinks, music and a nice view. The dress code is chic casual

Plunge - $$$
18 9th Avenue
The rooftop bar at the Hotel Gansevoort serves drinks, appetizers as well as a beautiful view.

Tao Downtown Nightclub - $$$
369 W 16th Street
The beautiful restaurant is also home to one of the coolest nightclubs in the area

PH-D Rooftop Lounge no hotel Dream Downtown -$$$$
355 W 16th Street
Located on the twelfth floor of the Dream Downtown hotel and with a wonderful view of the city, it is a good choice for a happy hour or night out.

 MoMA *(NY Modern Art Museum - 11 W 53rd St | **www.moma.org**)* offers free entry on Fridays between 4 pm and 8pm, but there is usually a line and it is more crowded inside.

Morgan Library and Museum *(225 Madison Ave | **www.themorgan.org**)* is free on Fridays between 2 pm and 5 pm.

New York Hall of Science (47-01 111th St | nysci.org) is free on Fridays between 3 pm and 5 pm.

SATURDAY

I would give the greatest sunset in the world for one sight of New York's skyline.

Ayn Rand

If you are not a fan of street food or night life, you can follow this itinerary on any other weekday (Monday and Tuesday perhaps?!) to avoid lines and crowds on the bridge.

You can also change the order to start the day in Williamsburg if you wish and end the day around Brooklyn Bridge Park/DUMBO to catch a beautiful sunset facing downtown Manhattan and the Brooklyn Bridge. You can get from Williamsburg to Dumbo by taking **the NYC ferry as seen on page 152.**

 To see free options for this day, see **page 155**.

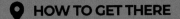

HOW TO GET THERE

 Subways **4** **5** **6** **R** **W** **J** **Z** to **Brooklyn Bridge/City Hall**.

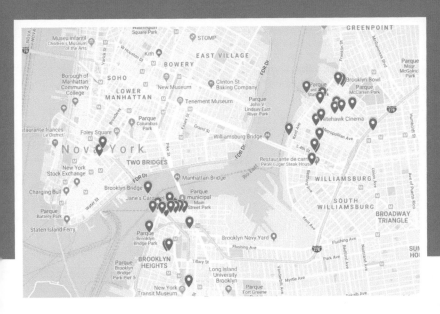

SUGGESTED BREAKFAST

• **Starbucks**
38 Park Row #4
Chosen based on the location from where we are starting the day.

BROOKLYN BRIDGE, DUMBO AND BROOKLYN HEIGHTS

1 **TODAY WE WILL BE BUSY!**
Let's start with the Brooklyn Bridge/City Hall area. That's where you will also find several government buildings and the Marriage Bureau, where thousands of couples say yes to love every year.

■ From there, we'll head to the famous Brooklyn Bridge. Yes, we will cross it by foot! But if you wish, it is possible to rent one of the Citi bikes close by as well and cross the bridge by bike. The daily pass is $15 or you can get a single pass for $3.50. You need to renew the rental every 30 minutes.

■ If you don't feel like crossing the entire bridge, take the subway **2** **3** (*Clark Street Station*), **F** (*York Street*) or the **A** **C** (*High Street Station*) to Brooklyn.

2 After crossing, we will arrive in the heart of DUMBO! Did you know that the name is a geographical abbreviation that stands for Down Under the Manhattan Bridge Overpass?

3 The first stop is the intersection of Washington Street and Water Street where you can see the famous view of the Manhattan Bridge - with the Empire State Building right in the center- it gets photographed hundreds of times a day. If you find it difficult to locate it, look up **41 Washington Street** on your GPS.

TIP
If you love bookstores, **Powerhouse books** (*32 Adams St)* is a great place to stop! Their NYC and children's book sections are great!

TIP
Dumbo Archway (*155 Water St)* Many events take place under this arch all year long, especially in the summer!

4 From there, keep going straight towards the bridge and turn left onto *Plymouth Street*, you'll pass by a visitor center (restroom available) and stairs that lead to a beautiful view of the Manhattan Bridge and to your left the famous pebble "beach", a place to sit and enjoy the view of Manhattan and the Brooklyn Bridge.There is also a nice playground if you are traveling with kids right next to it (towards Plymouth).

5 From there, head to Empire Stores, a complex of shops, offices, a museum, and some nice restaurants! It's also home of the popular Timeout Market, with several eateries handpicked by the magazine and website editors. Get on the elevator to go up to the top floor to have a beautiful view of the city and more food and drink options!

🍪 SUGGESTIONS FOR BREAKFAST

One Girl Cookies - $
33 Main Street
Cupcakes, cakes, cookies and more!

Bluestone lane - $
55 Prospect Street
Avocado toast and great coffee!? You got it!

Dumbo Market - $
66 Front Market
For those who enjoy the idea of having a picnic by the river, you could buy everything here!

Almondine Bakery - $
85 Water Street
The best of French pâtisserie in the heart of Dumbo

Clinton St. Baking Company - Time Out Market - $$
55 Water St
Their traditional brunch is delicious.

6 From there, stop by **Jane's Carousel** (*Old Dock Street - $2*). Kids love it - and adults do too! The Carousel doesn't operate every day, check the days and schedule on *www. janescarousel.com*

7 From there, just walk around and end the day around Pier 1 with a beautiful view of downtown Manhattan. The **Squibb Park Bridge** and the **Pier 1 Salt Marsh** are two other spots for beautiful pictures nearby!

 **WHERE TO EAT**

Jacques Torres Chocolate - $
66 Water Street
Chocolates, cookies and ice cream.

Grimaldi's Pizza - $$
1 Front Street
One of the most famous pizzas in NY.
Payment only in cash and only pies -
they don't sell slices.

Odd Fellows Ice Cream Co. - $ to $$
44 Water Street

Time Out Market - $ to $$
55 Water Street
Several eateries under one roof.

Shake Shack - $ to $$
1 Old Fulton Street
Beloved NYC fast food

The River Café - $$$$
1 Water Street
One of the most romantic restaurants,
sophisticated and with a beautiful view!

Cecconi's - $$$
55 Water Street
Modern classic Italian with waterfront
views, right by the East River.

Celestine Dumbo - $$ to $$$
1 John Street
Eatern Mediterranean restaurant with a
beautiful view of Manhattan Bridge.

NEXT STOP: WILLIAMSBURG!

This is known as the hipster neighborhood in Brooklyn, it has that local vibe we love. But it became very trendy and popular over the years and new businesses are popping up every now and then, so it's always a good idea to go back if you've been there before!

The best way to explore Williamsburg is by walking around. I'll leave some suggestions for places, shops and restaurants to see but pay close attention and choose what is more to your taste before you go to create your own itinerary today. You can explore the entire area by foot, you just need energy and comfortable shoes!

 HOW TO GET THERE

 At Pier 1 on **Brooklyn Bridge Park**, take the NYC ferry ($2.75) to **North Williamsburg** OR if you want to stop by **Domino Park** (page 153), get off at **South Williamsburg**.

 From Manhattan you can take the Ⓛ train towards Brooklyn and get off at Bedford Avenue station.

Smorgasburg

If you are taking the ferry and it's a Saturday between April and November (check website for official dates) from 11am - 6pm, you can start exploring the area by heading to Smorgasburg and trying some of the delicious local food vendors by the river.

- **Saturdays in Williamsburg**
  East River State Park | 90 Kent Ave. (at N. 7 St.)
- **Sundays at Prospect Park**
  Prospect Park – Breeze Hill | East Drive at Lincoln Rd.

In the winter the location changes, check the official website for the schedule and updated address: *www.smorgasburg.com*

Domino Park | *300 Kent Ave*

Built on the Williamsburg waterfront in front of Domino, a defunct sugar factory, the park, which bears the same name, attracts tourists and locals year-round. In summer, it's the right choice to enjoy the end of the day, play (in the sand !!), let the kids free on the playground and admire the beautiful view of Manhattan!

Artists and Fleas | *70 North 7th Street*

A market which opens on weekends and brings together works of designers, collectors and various artists who sell a bit of everything.
Open every weekend from 10AM - 7PM | *www.artistsandfleas.com/williamsburg*

Brooklyn Brewery | *9 North 11th Street*

You can tour the famous Brooklyn brewery. Only 21 with identification can consume alcoholic beverages. *www.brooklynbrewery.com*

Brooklyn Flea Market

Brooklyn's famous flea market takes place on Saturdays in Williamsburg *(51 N 6th Street)* and Sundays on DUMBO *(80 Pearl Street)*. Check the official website for updates on locations and hours: ***www.brooklynflea.com***

THRIFT STORES

If you enjoy thrift stores, there are some nice ones in Williamsburg:

- **Crossroads Trading** | *135 N 7th St*
- **Buffalo Exchange** | *504 Driggs Ave*
- **Beacon's Closet** | *74 Guernsey Street*

Now it's time to explore the other side of Williamsburg! If you are arriving in Brooklyn by train you can simply use your GPS to get to the places suggested in the first part of the itinerary.

SOME THINGS TO SEE AND DO

1 Bedford Avenue is full of local shops, cafés, and restaurants. Driggs and Manhattan Avenue are also worth exploring as well! Put some of the addresses listed here on Google Maps or discover your new favorites!

2 **Mini Mall** *(218 Bedford Ave)*
A space for local vendors, bookstore, coffee shop, thrift store and more!

3 **Figureworks** *(168 North 6th Street | www.figureworks.com)*
An art gallery in Williamsburg.

4 **Nitehawk Cinema** *(136 Metropolitan Ave)*
If you are in the mood for an independent movie, check out this space! They serve food and drinks before, during and after the movies.

🍽 WHERE TO EAT

The Rabbit Hole - $$
352 Bedford Avenue
Delicious food, drinks, and vintage atmosphere. Good for brunch!

Surf Bar - $ to $$
139 N 6th Street
Delicious food and decor inspired by Hawaii. There's even sand on the floor!

Martha's Country Bakery - $
175 Bedford Ave
Cakes, pies, cheesecakes, cookies and more! Vegan options available!

Kings County Imperial - $$
20 Skillman Avenue
Chinese-American cuisine in a unique environment.

Woops! - $
548 Driggs Ave
Coffee shop with different branches but this is my favorite.

The Bagel Store - $
754 Metropolitan Ave
Where the famous rainbow bagel was born! They serve different types of bagels and cream cheese fillings!

Little Choc Apothecary - $ to $$
141 Havemeyer Street
The 1st NY café with a totally gluten-free and vegan menu! The crepes are very yummy!

Wholefoods
238 Bedford Avenue
Organic supermarket with plenty of gluten, and vegan options.

Brooklyn Winery - $$
213 N 8th St
Local wine producers offering also beer and a few bites.

Roberta's - $$
6 Grand Street, Brooklyn
Delicious wood fired Neapolitan pizza, salads and baked goods.

🍸 ROOFTOP BARS

They are close to each other:

Westlight - The William Vale Hotel
111 N 12th St 22nd floor

The Water Tower Bar - Williamsburg Hotel
96 Wythe Ave

 At the **Solomon R. Guggenheim Museum** (*1071 5th Ave | www.guggenheim.org*), on Saturdays between 4 pm and 6 pm you pay what you wish. Suggested admission is $10.

The **Jewish Museum** (*1109 5th Ave & E 92nd St | thejewishmuseum.org*) is free on Saturdays.

♕ NIGHTLIFE IN THE AREA

If you like live music or a good party, here are some of the best of Williamsburg.

Brooklyn Bowl - $$
61 Wythe Avenue
www.brooklynbowl.com
A fun bowling alley with a bar and live music every night. There is a cover charge (check the website for updates). By day it's a great place for families who like bowling. The bowling alley costs $25/30min for up to 8 people (2019). The shoe rental has an additional cost of $4.95 per person. They also serve drinks and food.

Freehold
45 South 3rd Street
Live music, comedy bar and fun parties

The Whiskey Brooklyn
44 Berry Street
Bar and underground night club.

Brooklyn Billiards
90 North 11th Street
Play, drink and eat, all in one place.

Music Hall of Williamsburg
66 N 6th Street
It has shows most nights of the week.

Baby's All Right
146 Broadway
Live music most nights, gourmet bar fare, drinks and brunch on weekends.

Radegast Hall and Biergarten
113 North 3rd Street
Beer hall and live music (check the website for updated schedule: radegasthall.com)

MORE PLACES TO EAT IN WILLIAMSBURG

Sea Wolf - $$ to $$$
420 Kent Ave, Brooklyn, NY
Seafood and great views!

Diner - $$
85 Broadway, Brooklyn, NY
The menu changes almost daily and
you can dine inside a 90 year old
Pullman dining car.

Aurora - $$
70 Grand St, Brooklyn, NY
Great and beautiful Italian restaurant.

Devoción Coffee - $
69 Grand St, Brooklyn, NY
For coffee lovers!

Gelateria Gentile - $
253 Wythe Ave, Brooklyn, NY
One of the best gelatos in Italy (and of
course, Williamsburg!)

Bakeri - $
150 Wythe Ave, Brooklyn, NY
A nice spot for coffee and pastries.

It is ridiculous to set a detective story in New York City. New York City is itself a detective story.

Agatha Christie

SUNDAY

Queens Botanical Gardens
43-50 Main St | queensbotanical.org
Free from April to October on Sundays between 9 am and 11 am. And free on any day between November and March.

HOW TO GET THERE

Subways **2** **3** **A** **C** **B**
and get off at **116 Street**.

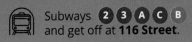

SUGGESTED BREAKFAST

• Levain Bakery
2167 Frederick Douglass Boulevard
One of New York's most famous cookies!

• Il Caffe Latte
189 Malcolm X Blvd # 1

1 Located in Upper Manhattan, Harlem is a large neighborhood with many cool spots to visit! I selected some places that I believe are worth visiting if you have an extra day in the city.

2 Harlem has become world-famous for its gospel choirs during regular services and some churches offer special musical performances during the Christmas season. For an updated schedule check the official websites

■ You should keep in mind that the atmosphere inside is respectful and the locals who frequent the churches don't enjoy the distraction of tourists who are passing by. So, make sure that photos and videos are allowed before you start recording everything with your camera, right?

TIP

The **Brooklyn Tabernacle Church** *(17 Smith St)* also has one of the most beautiful choirs in NY. Their Christmas show is becoming more popular every year!

TIP

Want to go shopping? In Harlem, you'll find a nice variety of shops like Burlington Coat Factory, Marshalls, H&M, Target and even a Whole Foods!

CHURCHES WITH A GOSPEL CHOIR

First Corinthian Baptist Church
1912 Adam Clayton Powell Jr. Blvd., 116th St | fcbcnyc.org

Bethel Gospel Assembly
2 E 120th St #26 | www.bethelga.org

The Abyssinian Baptist Church
132 W 138th St
One of the most famous in NY. *www. abyssinian.org*

Canaan Baptist Church
132 W 116th St| www.bethelga.org

TIP

After the services I recommend dining at one of the most popular restaurants in Harlem for brunch on Sundays: Sylvia's Restaurant and Amy Ruth's! But if you can't there are plenty of places around!

3 I suggest a visit to the iconic **Apollo Theater** *(253 W 125th St)*, originally called **Hurtig & Seamon's New Burlesque Theater**. The theater opened in 1914 and, like several establishments from that period, it only allowed white people. In 1934, its name changed to Apollo and the burlesque shows were replaced by various types of performances (jazz, comedy shows). Many iconic artists have performed on the stage and still continues till this day. If you wish, you can take a guided tour in the theater, book through the website: *www.apollotheater.org/event/historic-tours/*

4 If you have time and wish to check out some local art, **The Studio Museum in Harlem** *(144 West 125th Street | www.studiomuseum.org)* is a good choice. It was founded in 1968 and is known internationally for promoting the work of artists descended from Africa with several cool exhibitions. It only operates from Thursday to Sunday. Tickets cost $7 for adults (2019), $3 for students or over 65 and free for children under 12. Admission on Sundays is free.

5 If you need a break, you can stop at the **Marcus Garvey Park** *(18 Mt Morris Park W)* to relax for a bit! But don't forget that the neighborhood is huge, and you can spend a whole day only exploring its history, shops, restaurants and museums.

TIP

NiLu *(191 Malcolm X Blvd | shopnilu.com)* is a beautiful Harlem store where you not only find unique items and gifts, but you also can better understand the region through the eyes and works of local artists.

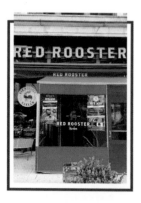

🍽 WHERE TO EAT

Sylvia's Restaurant- $$
328 Malcolm X Blvd
An icon of the region, perfect for Sundays brunches.

Amy Ruth's - $$
113 W 116th St | amyruths.com
With traditional food like Sylvia's but usually with a shorter line.

BLV Bistro - $$
2149 Frederick Douglass Blvd | boulevardbistrony.com
A cozy atmosphere also offers cocktails and wines.

Uptown Veg - $$
52 E 125th St
Vegan restaurant with traditional food per pound, in addition to natural juices and smoothies.

Red Rooster - $$
310 Malcolm X Blvd
www.redroosterharlem.com
Chef Marcus Samuelsson's restaurant. The place is modern, fun and busy on Sundays! And in the basement, you can watch live performances. Check out the website for details.

Harlem Shake - $$
100 W 124th St
www.harlemshakenyc.com
Burger, milkshakes and other classic American diners in a casual and retro atmosphere.

Corner Social - $$
321 Lenox Ave
www.cornersocialnyc.com
Bar and restaurant. There is also a DJ on some nights.

TIP

Free Tours by Foot offers comprehensive guided tours of Harlem as well! Check the website before you go. The tours are free, but you pay a tip at the end if you like the experience! They offer tours in English and Spanish!

IF YOU FEEL LIKE YOU WANT A DIFFERENT SUGGESTION ON WHAT TO VISIT ON A SUNDAY IN UPTOWN, HERE ARE A FEW:

The Met Cloisters | *99 Margaret Corbin Drive, Fort Tryon Park*
This museum is located north of Fort Tryon Park in Uptown, on the west side and next to the Hudson River. Part of the Metropolitan Museum of Art. Ticket price is $25 per adult and the ticket is also valid for the Metropolitan Museum on 5th Avenue and The Met Breuer and vice versa.

El Museo Del Barrio | *1230 5th Avenue*
Dedicated to Latin culture in general, with a shop and a cafe with traditional delights! Suggested price: $9 per adult, $5 for students and over 65. Free for children under 12 years. It operates
from Wednesday to Sunday except on national holidays.

The Cathedral Church of St. John the Divine | *1047 Amsterdam Avenue at 112th Street*
With over 120 years, the cathedral is amazing and has masses during the week as well.

Columbia University | *116th St & Broadway*
Founded in 1754 this is the oldest university in NYC and 5th oldest in the country. Columbia University has its campus in Upper Manhattan and is worth the visit!

OR IF YOU ARE IN THE MOOD FOR MIDTOWN...

HUDSON YARDS | THE EDGE THE VESSEL

Head to **Hudson Yards**, a residential and commercial complex that includes a shopping mall with incredible restaurants and **Little Spain**, a Spanish food court. You will also find **The Shed,** an amazing art center for different exhibitions, performances and much more. Right next to it you will see **The Vessel**, a modern sculpture with about 2,500 steps. You can also go up to the **Edge**, the highest outdoor sky deck in the Western Hemisphere. If you haven't been to the **High Line Park**, it ends or starts right by The Shops (the mall)! Check the first Sunday itinerary for more information about Hudson Yards!

To get there
Subway 7 to *Hudson Yards*.

MONDAY

New York is really the place to be; to go to New York, you're going to the center of the world, the lion's den.

Zubin Mehta

 HOW TO GET THERE

Subways **7 M G E**
and get off at **Court Square Station**.

NYC ferry - Long Island City or **Hunters Point South**

SUGGESTED BREAKFAST

· Court Square Diner
45-30 23rd St
A traditional retro diner since 1946. It operates 24 hours a day. The diner has been a set for TV series and movies such as *Jessica Jones, Gotham, Person of Interest, Blue Bloods, etc.*

🎯 DID YOU KNOW?

Queens is the place for having an authentic international dining experience!

- **Flushing**
  An even larger version of Chinatown with several restaurants and shops. Great to shop for beauty products and cheaper food, clothing and groceries.

- **Elmhurst**
  For Thai, Vietnamese, Chinese restaurants and more, this is the place!

- **Jackson Heights**
  For Indian and Latin food lovers, a stop in Jackson Heights is a must. They say the best Mexican tacos are here!

- **Astoria**
  An eclectic culinary mix from every corner of the world, it is home to the largest Greek Community outside of Greece. There you can also find several Brazilian restaurants in different parts, as well as Arabic restaurants and shops.

1 **FIRST STOP OF THE DAY: EXPLORE THE MOMA MUSEUM PS1**

If you decide to take the train, a visit to the Museum of Modern Art extension, the **MoMA PS1** *(22-25 Jackson Avenue | www.moma.org/visit)* is an opportunity to get out of the obvious and explore this part of New York that keeps growing by the minute. In addition to the exhibitions, several events take place there during the year. There is a suggested entrance fee (U$10), but you pay what you wish.

The museum is closed on Tuesdays and Wednesdays.

■ **PS: If you are not in the mood for the museum or the diner,** I suggest taking the NYC ferry (U\$2.75) instead for a nice view of the city. There are two ferry stations in the area: Long Island City or Hunters Point South. You can buy your ticket on the NYC ferry app. Check out the spots and map for boarding on: *www.ferry.nyc*

2 From there head to the beautiful **Gantry Plaza State Park** *(4-09 47th Rd)*, a park with a beautiful view of Manhattan. It takes about 10 minutes to walk towards the center of the park and you can see how this area is different from most places in NYC.

■ In addition to one of the nicest and closest views of Manhattan, in the park, you'll also find the iconic 1940 Pepsi-Cola sign that is now officially a New York City landmark and a fun photo op as well. There was an old Pepsi (obviously) factory and, even after its closure, it continued as a symbol of the industrial era that was part of Queens not too distant history.

■ The park is a great place to go with kids, there is a playground and a grass area to relax, have a picnic and enjoy the view - or even exercise!

■ **Queens Public Library at Hunters Point**
47-40 Center Blvd
If you have time, stop by the beautiful and modern library of Long Island City.

■ **The Gutter LIC**
10-22 46th Avenue | www.thegutterbarles.com
It is a vintage bowling bar and a great idea for a very relaxed happy hour in the area. You must be over 21 to enter.

Fan of rock climbing? You can attend a rock climbing class at **The Cliffs at LIC** (*11-11 44th Dr. | lic.thecliffsclimbing. com*). It costs about $30/day.

■ **Socrates Sculpture Park**
32-01 Vernon Boulevard | socratessculpturepark.org
For those who enjoy art and sculpture, Socrates Sculpture Park is free for all year round.

Next to Socrates Sculpture Park is the **Noguchi Museum**, which was created by the sculptor Isamu Noguchi and opened to the public in 1985 to preserve and publicize his works. The museum also has a beautiful garden with some works by the artist. Unfortunately it doesn't open on Mondays and Tuesdays. Admission is $ 10 per adult and $ 5 for adults over 65 or students. *www.noguchi.org*

WHERE TO EAT

LIC Landing - $
52-10 Center Blvd
A cafe in the same park by the river serving snacks and drinks with a beautiful view!

Bareburger - $$
48-19 Vernon Boulevard
Organic and great burgers, salads and appetizers. Vegan options available.

Skinny's Cantina - $$
4704 Center Boulevard
Popular mexican restaurant in the area.

SHI - $$
4720 Center Blvd
Upscale pan-asian restaurant.

American Brass - $$$
2-01 50th Ave, Queens, NY
An upscale waterfront restaurant by Chef Kevin McGinley. Make sure you check the seafood options.

Fifty Hammer Brewing - $
10-28 46th Avenue
www.fifthhammerbrewing.com
A brewery with live music (check out website calendar) in the heart of Long Island City.

Casa Enrique - $$
5-48 49th Ave
For authentic Mexican food!

Blvd Wine Bar - $
4720 Center Blvd
Wines, champagne, cocktails, beers, artisanal cheeses and other appetizers. Drinks cost on average $5-8. They also serve brunch on weekends.

Rockaway Brewing Company - $
46-01 5th Street
rockawaybrewco.com
Handcrafted beer factory that started in Rockaway and a few years ago expanded to Long Island City.

How about a picnic in the park?
In the warmer months you will find food trucks around the park or you can stop by Food Cellar Market for groceries. In the summer of 2021 a Trader Joe's is due to open in the area. *(4-85 47th Road)*

TIP

There are several events in the neighborhood especially in the summer, including movie nights! Check the website for more information and calendar schedule:
www.hunterspointparks.org

3 If you have enough time, I recommend staying in the park for sunset and watching the city lights come to life . From there you can either take the ferry back to Manhattan or if you prefer to explore another area in Queens, I recommend going to Ditmars in Astoria to experience more of the local atmosphere and traditional Greek cuisine in one of the most authentic areas.

4 To get there from Long Island City just take the **7** train towards **Queens/Flushing** and transfer at Queensborough Plaza to the subway line **N** **W** (towards Astoria). It takes about 10 minutes to get to the last stop where you will get off (Astoria Ditmars Blvd). Once you are there, walk towards Ditmars Boulevard and check out the many restaurants and shops around the area!

🍽 WHERE TO EAT GREEK FOOD IN ASTORIA

Taverna Kyclades - $$
33-07 Ditmars Blvd
Usually there is a line to get in.

Stamatis - $$
29-09 23rd Ave
Another classic in Astoria, a family-friendly spot for hearty Greek staples in a simple setting.

Elia's Corner - $$
24-02 31st St
Grilled fresh fish is the specialty here.
Cash only.

WHERE TO EAT SWEETS IN ASTORIA

Chip - $
22-04 33rd Street
Delicious cookies!

Fresh Start Organic Market and Eatery - $
29-13 23rd Avenue
Organic treats, groceries, natural juice, etc.

Dough Doughnuts - $
21-70 31st Street
Tasty and unique flavored doughnuts.

New York City Bagel and Coffee House - $
2908 23rd Avenue
Great bagels and pastries.
Delicious cookies!

Martha's Country Bakery - $
36-21 Ditmars Blvd
Desserts, desserts and wait...desserts!

👤 DID YOU KNOW?

This area is also close to **Astoria Park**, a park by the river with plenty of space to run, practice sports, there is a playground for children and a free community pool in the summer. If you are going during the day it is worth checking it out.

TIP

If you are in the mood and are interested in technology, TV and cinema, I recommend checking out the **Museum of the Moving Image** *(36-01 35 Ave | www.movingimage.us)* in Astoria. The entrance is $15 per adult (2020) and free on Fridays between 4 pm and 8 pm.

How to get there: Metro R M and get off at Steinway Street OR the N W and get off on station *36 Avenue* station.

WHERE TO EAT IN THE MUSEUM AREA

This area has many restaurants but if you want to stay close to the train and If you feel like trying japanese fusion food with a nice view of Queens and Manhattan I recommend **Luna Asian Bistro** *(32-72 Steinway St 6th fl | www.lunaasianbistro.com).*

If you have more time and are interested, I recommend exploring the 30th Avenue and Broadway areas where you will find more shops and great restaurants.

TUESDAY

A hundred times I have thought: New York is a catastrophe, and fifty times: it is a beautiful catastrophe.

Le Corbusier

HOW TO GET THERE

Take the **PATH Train**
and get off at **Hoboken** station.

SUGGESTED BREAKFAST

• **La Casa**
54 Newark Street

• **Starbucks**
51 Newark St

HOBOKEN

A beautiful port town, important to the development of the country and known as the home of Frank Sinatra and baseball, Hoboken is the perfect option to slow down from the madness that New York might be at times and enjoy a quieter atmosphere. The city has an amazing view facing the Hudson River and the New York skyline.

1

FIRST STOP

If you are a fan of the reality show Cake Boss when leaving the station go to **Carlo's Bake Shop** *(95 Washington St),* where the reality show was shot and one of the most visited places in Hoboken by tourists and fans of the show. There you'll find plenty of treats, such as cakes and pastries, as well as the traditional cannolis! Across the street, you'll find the **Hoboken City Hall**.

TIP

Around there you can also find the **Fire Department Museum** *(213 Bloomfield Street)*, which is open on weekends. A great tip for anyone traveling with kids. It costs $3 per adult (2020) and it is free for children.

2 From here, if you have time and are interested in fully exploring Hoboken, head to the **Hoboken Historical Museum** *(1301 Hudson St)* along Washington Street, the busiest street in town, where you will find several shops and restaurants. It takes about 20-25 minutes to walk to the museum! The museum costs $4 and isn't open on Mondays.

The Hoboken Museum Website *(www.hobokenmuseum.org)* offers a road map for anyone who wants to learn about all the city's spots and the history behind each one.

3 Head to **Castle Point Observation Terrace** followed by Frank Sinatra Park, Stevens Park, and Pier C Park, for a gorgeous Manhattan view! Over there, you'll also see a small memorial for soldiers from World War II.

If you are traveling with children, there is a playground at Pier C.

4 Before coming back, you can end the day at Pier A, where you also find a small memorial to the soldiers of the Vietnam War and First World War, millions of fighters have passed through Hoboken to embark on their battle destinations.

5 Close to Pier A, you'll also see the Hoboken maritime, rail and bus terminal, the **Erie-Lackawanna Terminal.**

Feel free to explore some of the many restaurants around town:

 WHERE TO EAT

La Casa - $ to $$
54 Newark Street
A small restaurant serving breakfast, brunch and other delights from Latin cuisine. Meat empanadas are among the top picks and they cost about $2 each.

Zack's - $$
232 Willow Ave
Hamburger, fries, pasta and a cool atmosphere. They also serve brunch!

Union Hall - $$
306 Sinatra Dr
Snacks, sandwiches, salads, drinks and more with a nice view of the Hudson River.

Insomnia Cookies - $
56 Newark Street
Very tasty cookies. There are other locations in New York City as well.

Halifax - $$$
225 River Street
American food, seafood, and brunch on weekends.

Pilsener Haus & Biergarten - $ to $$
1422 Grand St
Want to enjoy summer in Hoboken like a local? Head to this beer garden for drinks and some appetizers.

6 From there head back to the Path Train station entrance to return to New York or explore New Jersey's surroundings:

If you are in the mood for shopping, head to **Newport Centre Mall** *(30 Mall Dr W)*, a mall with a good variety of shops and restaurants.

How to get there: Take the PATH Train to **Journal Square** and get off at the **Newport** station then walk about 10 minutes.

Newark

It's a city with a large Brazilian and Portuguese community. You can find traditional restaurants, bakeries and stores selling imported goods for a good price.

Where to eat? Brasilia Grill, Delícias de Minas, Altas Horas Lanches, Casa Nova Grill...

Como chegar: Take the PATH train from Hoboken or from NY to Newark ($2.75) or take the New Jersey Transit, check the website for schedules: *www.njtransit.com*

Elizabeth - The Mills at Jersey Gardens *(651 Kapkowski Rd)*

The famous shopping and outlet mall in New Jersey.

Getting there departing from Hoboken: Check Google maps for best routes when you are there.

How to get to The Mills at Jersey Gardens from Manhattan:

Bus # 111 or # 115 from *Port Authority Bus Terminal*

Schedule and more information: *www.njtransit.com*

It takes about half an hour and it costs $14 round trip. You can buy the tickets at the machines in the station. Ask to get off at the Jersey Gardens stop.

IKEA *(1000 Ikea Dr)*

Shop for furniture, home decor and some other random items. You can also eat there.

Directions: Take bus # 111 from Manhattan and drop off at the Ikea store.

Walmart *(150 Harrison Ave)*

Supermarket with competitive prices in Kearny, NJ.

How to get there: The easiest way if you are in New Jersey is by taking a taxi or Uber from Newark or check Google maps for best routes when you are there.

I was in love with New York. I do not mean 'love' in any colloquial way, I mean that I was in love with the city, the way you love the first person who ever touches you and never love anyone quite that way again.

Joan Didion

WEDNESDAY

The Bronx is not on everyone's itinerary but there are some really interesting places to visit! So if you want to fully explore NYC I highly recommend paying a visit. Not all points of interest have access to the subway but you can easily walk or take a cab/Uber.

 ## HOW TO GET THERE

 Subway **D** to **161 Street Yankee Stadium Station**

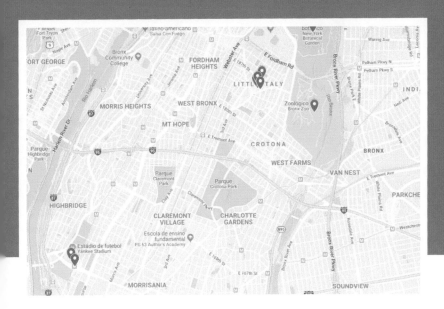

SUGGESTED BREAKFAST

 • Dunkin' Donuts
50 E 161st St

1 Since the Bronx has different places to visit and they are kind of spread out, I'll make some suggestions of what to do around there, simply choose what sounds most exciting to you:

Start the day around 11 am with a tour of the iconic Yankee Stadium and then head to Little Italy for lunch.

▓ YANKEE STADIUM

How to get there: **D** 161 Street - Yankee Stadium Station *(1 E 161st St)*

How about exploring **Yankee Stadium** a bit more with a full tour (in English and some in Spanish) to learn more about the stadium and New York's most famous baseball team? The tour lasts about an hour and a new one leaves every 20 minutes - starting at 11 am. The regular ticket costs about $20. You can also buy a combo which includes the tour and lunch at Hard Rock Cafe.
www.mlb.com/yankees/ballpark/tours

2 Little Italy, New York Botanical Garden, and the Bronx Zoo are quite near if you manage to exit and enter at the closest gates. You can walk from one to another. It shouldn't take you longer than 15-20 minutes.

▓ LITTLE ITALY

How to get there: **D** **B** to Fordham Road stop and walk of about 15 minutes.

The most authentic and least touristy Little Italy is on Arthur Avenue in the Bronx! There you'll find restaurants, local markets and everything related to Italian cuisine, shared through generations. Arthur Avenue is the busiest area and can be accessed by subway (Fordham Road Station) with another 15-20 minutes walk or by bus or Metro-North.

Where to eat in Little Italy? There are many options but let me break it down a little: **Mario's Restaurant** ($$ - 2342 Arthur Avenue), or **Zero Otto Nove** ($$ - 2357 Arthur Avenue), **Enzo's Of Arthur Avenue** ($$ - 2339 Arthur Avenue) or **Arthur Avenue Retail Market** ($-$$ - 2344 Arthur Ave).

3 The Bronx is home to many special places such as the **Botanical Garden of New York** *(2900 Southern Blvd)*. And for those who just want to take a look, admission is free every Wednesday and Saturday from 9 am to 10 am with access to the open garden area, it excludes attractions and special exhibitions. The regular ticket price is between $23-28 per adult. Great events happen there all year round and it is a great option for those traveling with children! Learn more here: *www.nybg.org*

▓ NEW YORK BOTANICAL GARDEN

How to get there: **B** **D** **4** *(Bedford Park Blvd station)* or **2** *(Allerton Avenue station)*. But you'll have to walk a bit. See all the options to get there here: *www.nybg.org/visit/directions/ | 2900 Southern Blvd*

TIP

From April to November you can check out the Bronx Night Market on Saturdays, an open space at Fordham Plaza to celebrate the city's cultural and gastronomic diversity. You will find several food stands and activities for the whole family, including events and music shows.

▓ BRONX ZOO

How to get there: take the **2** train and get off at Pelham Parkway and walk for about 10 minutes. Head towards the Zoo's Bronx River Entrance (Gate B).

OR take one of the buses that go there from Manhattan (BxM1), Bronx (Bx9 or Bx19 buses to 183rd Street and Southern Blvd OR take the Bx12 or Bx22 buses to Fordham Road and Southern Blvd) or you can also take a bus if you are coming from some parts of Queens (Q44 to 180th Street and Boston Road and then walk to the gate). See all public transportation options and details here: *bronxzoo.com/visitor-info/getting-here/transit*

The **Bronx Zoo** *(2300 Southern Boulevard)* is huge and offers year-round activities, events and attractions. Some are seasonal (such as butterfly garden, train ride, and children's zoo). Tickets cost between $20-30 and admission to children under 2 is free. Learn more here: *bronxzoo.com*

About

> *When I'm in New York, I just want to walk down the street and feel this thing, like I'm in a movie.*
>
> **Ryan Adams**

THURSDAY

Today is dedicated to exploring Prospect Park and its surroundings in Brooklyn. With a more serene atmosphere, this is one of the up and coming neighborhoods in Brooklyn, especially for families. Depending on your pace, you can spend an afternoon or even a full day in the area, especially if you are going with children.

HOW TO GET THERE

 Subway **2** **3** to **Grand Army Plaza**.

SUGGESTED BREAKFAST

 • **Tom's Restaurant**
782 Washington Ave

1 GRAND ARMY PLAZA

Start the day around **Grand Army Plaza**, at the **Soldiers' and Sailors' Memorial Arch**, completed in 1892 and the entrance to **Prospect Park**.

IN THIS AREA THERE IS A LOT TO BE EXPLORED

2 BROOKLYN BOTANICAL GARDEN

455 Flatbush Avenue | www.bbg.org
The Brooklyn botanical garden is a must visit especially in the spring, when the flowers and the beautiful cherry trees are in bloom. The Japanese garden is one of my favorite places there. The ticket costs U $ 18 per adult. They used to offer free admission on Fridays and other days of the week in the winter, but in 2021 this service was suspended and replaced by the community ticket, which are free tickets for people who cannot pay the amount charged. But check the website for updates.

3 **PROSPECT PARK**

Introduced in 1867 and designed by the creators of Central Park, Frederick Law Olmsted, and Calvert Vaux, Prospect Park remains one of the largest urban parks in the country with several interesting spots and an unmissable destination at all times of the year, especially in autumn when the trees look beautiful as they change colors.

WHAT TO SEE AROUND THERE:

- Prospect Park Lake;
- Long Meadow;
- Prospect Park Zoo;
- Carousel at the park's Children's Corner;
- Samuel J. and Ethel LeFrak Center at Lakeside - with an ice skating rink in colder months and other activities in the warmer seasons.
- Lefferts Historic House, a true journey back in time exploring the historic home built by a Dutch family in the 18th century. You can explore the garden, play with objects, etc ... There are various activities for children throughout the year.
- Boathouse, a gorgeous venue for events and weddings built in 1905.

BROOKLYN MUSEUM

200 Eastern Parkway | www.brooklynmuseum.org
With approximately 52,000 square feet, this art museum is one of the largest and oldest in the United States. Several educational activities and exhibitions take place there during the year, it is worth checking out if you like museums. It costs $16 per adult to get in but the price is suggested.

BROOKLYN PUBLIC LIBRARY

www.bklynlibrary.org
The 5th largest library in the United States, a good option to slow down and enjoy the local atmosphere.

Note: Prospect Park area is huge, so the distances might be long. I recommend planning where to eat before going there to save time and energy or simply use Yelp to find good options near you.

TIP

If you are traveling with children the **Brooklyn Children's Museum** is a great option for children aged 6 months to 10 years! The ticket costs $13 per person over the age of one, but you can pay whatever you want on Thursdays between 2:00 pm and 5:00 pm. *(145 Brooklyn Avenue, Brooklyn, NY)*. Another great activity for families is to explore the **Transit Museum** *(99 Schermerhorn Street)*. Admission is $ 10 per adult and $ 5 for children ages 2 to 17. More information on the website: *www.nytransitmuseum.org*

🍽 WHERE TO EAT

Chavela's - $$
736 Franklin Ave
It serves Mexican food in a relaxed setting near Prospect Park.

Silver Rice Sushi - $
638 Park Place
Sushi, rice bowls and they also serve sushi and other top choices in a cup, so you can take it wherever you want.

Greenwood Park - $$
555 7th Ave
A beer garden with outdoor and indoor space, food and good beer!

Terrace Bagels - $
222 &, 222A Prospect Park West
If you feel like having a traditional bagel, this is a good spot.

Ix Restaurant Food Coffee & Cacao - $ to $$
43 Lincoln Rd
Coffee shop serving delicious pastries, soups and other Guatemalan baked goods.

La Bagel Delight - $
284 7th Ave
Bagels, bagels and bagels!

Five Guys - $
284 7th Ave
Next to La Bagel Delight. Popular fast-food chain in NY! Locals love their fries and the free peanuts while you wait!

ARE YOU UP FOR SHOPPING?
To end the day, if you are in the mood for shopping, I suggest going to the **Atlantic Avenue/Barclays Center** *(625 Atlantic Ave)*, an area with cool shops outside and inside Atlantic Terminal Mall (such as Target, Party City, Bath and Body Works, TJ Maxx, Best Buy, Victoria's Secret), a mall located in front of Barclays Center, a famous event and sports arena in Brooklyn.

TIP
If you like bookstores, there is a **Barnes and Noble** in the Prospect Park area: *267 7th Ave.*

FRIDAY

London is satisfied,
Paris is resigned, but New
York is always hopeful.

Dorothy Parker

Coney Island has so much history and it's such a unique place in New York that if you have time, especially if traveling between May- September, I recommend taking the train and spending the day there! You will find an iconic amusement park, beach, boardwalk, aquarium and much more!

HOW TO GET THERE

Subways **N** **Q** **D** **F** to **Coney Island**.

NYC Ferry - Coney Island

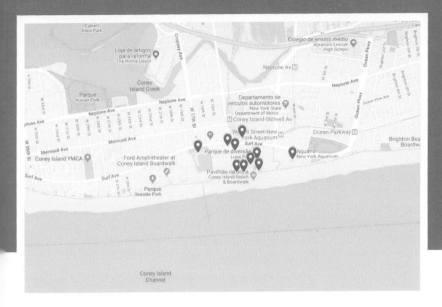

SUGGESTED BREAKFAST (OR LUNCH)

- **Tom's Coney Island**
1229 Boardwalk

My first glimpse of this park was watching the movie Uptown Girls, one of my favorite movies shot in New York!

1 The main attraction besides the beach is the iconic **Luna Park**, which is a great option for kids of all ages! It has that retro vibe inside the park that will take you back to your childhood! On Friday nights they also offer a fireworks show, which I LOVE! If you are going in the summer, avoid Saturdays and Sundays, when it usually gets super crowded!

For hours of operation check out the calendar on Luna Park's website to see the days and hours especially in September and October. The park doesn't open in the winter (from November to March).

2 Luna Park tickets: you should expect to spend an average of $20 to $65 per person, depending on the type of ticket you would like to buy (all day pass or pay per ride). You can buy tickets online or at the park. *lunaparknyc.com*

Oh! You can't ride **Deno's Wonder Wheel Amusement Park** attractions with a Luna Card, even though they are so close by.

FAN OF BASEBALL?
The MCU Park is home of Brooklyn Cyclones championship baseball and it is really close to Luna Park! Check the official website for games, tickets and other fun events! *www.brooklyncyclones.com*

🎙️ DID YOU KNOW?

On Independence Day (4th of July), Coney Island hosts a Hot Dog Eating Contest, where the competitors have to eat the most number of hot dogs in the least amount of time.

3 Be sure to stroll along the boardwalk to find several restaurants and diverse shops and places to eat. There you'll also find the famous **Nathan's Hot Dog** *(1310 Surf Ave)*. There is another branch on the beach promenade and other places in NY, but this is the most famous!

🧑 DID YOU KNOW?

The first roller coaster in the United States opened in 1884 on Coney Island. And today you can ride Cyclone, a wooden roller coaster debuted in 1927 and very fast! It's still one of the oldest in operation and one of the park's most popular rides.

💡 TIP

The Coney Island aquarium is a great option for families with children. Regular adult tickets cost $20.95 and U$16.95 for children but prices might change.
Admission on Wednesday afternoons is by pay-what-you-wish from 3:00pm to last entry. Check the official website for hours of operation as it changes according to the season.

🍽 WHERE TO EAT

Nathan's Famous - $
1310 Surf Avenue

Paul's Daughter - $
1001 Boardwalk

Rita's Italian Ice & Frozen Custard - $
1327 Surf Ave

Totonno's Pizzeria - $$
1524 Neptune Ave

TIP

Looking for a happy hour vibe?
I recommend the **Coney Island Brewery** *(1904 Surf Ave).*

WOULD YOU LIKE TO SEE MORE OF CONEY ISLAND?

Then check out some of the productions that took place there!

▦ **In the movies:** Brooklyn (2015), Uptown Girl (2003), Men in Black 3 (2012) and Wonder (2017).

▦ **In music:** Coney Island has appeared in several music clips, some of my favorites are: *Beyonce - XO, New Kids on the Block - Please Don't Go Girl* and *The Wanted - Lose my Mind.*

> *One can't paint New York as it is, but rather as it is felt.*
>
> **Georgia O'Keefe**

SATURDAY

Today is a day to explore a not so obvious part of Queens: Corona and Flushing!

📍 COMO CHEGAR

 Subway **7** to **111 Street Station**.

SUGGESTED BREAKFAST (OR LUNCH)

• **Queens Museum**
There is a small cafe inside the museum if you are interested.

1 Let's start the day in **Flushing Meadows Corona Park**, which bears the name of the two surrounding neighborhoods: **Flushing and Corona**.

2 In addition to being a very enjoyable green area there is plenty to see and do there, such as the **Queens Museum** (with a panoramic view of New York City in miniature that is worth checking out). Suggested price to enter the museum is $8, but you can pay what you want; the **NY Hall of Science; the Queens Theater; the Queens Zoo; the New York State Pavilion and the USTA Billie Jean King National Tennis Center**, where the **US Open** takes place annually.

Not so far from there, you will also find Citi Field, home of the New York Mets, a famous New York baseball team.

Overall, there are activities to do all year round in the area such as events, music festivals, and even the Queens Night Market, a great chance to experience the local life.

DID YOU KNOW?

The movie **MIB - Men in Black** had scenes shot at Flushing Meadows Corona Park! The globe was destroyed in the movie but it remains intact in the real world. This symbol is beautiful, made of stainless steel and was commissioned for the New York World's Fair of 1964 to celebrate the dawn of space and peace through understanding.

TIP

Jazz lover? Queens was home to several names in the music, including Louis Armstrong! The singer's house *(34-56 107th St)* is also a museum and fans can explore the inner and outer part of the house that was kept as it was, with furniture and some personal objects. During the tour, you can listen to the original music and audio from the artist's daily life. Tickets cost $12 per adult (2020). More information on *www.louisarmstronghouse.org*. Walking from and to the subway station (111th Street) should take you between 15 and 20 minutes.

3 Towards the end of the day walk or take subway **7** again but now to the end of the line, to Main Street, also in Flushing, known for its vibrant chinese community. I love exploring this neighborhood! There you can find several shops and restaurants serving food from various parts of China and South Korea among others. The subway ride or walk takes about 20 minutes depending on what part of the park you are in.

SHOPPING TIP

If you don't want to continue the trip to Main Street but feel like shopping, the Queens Center Mall (90-15 Queens Blvd) is a traditional mall with all the most popular stores plus several restaurants, including The Cheesecake Factory, one of my favorite restaurants chains. To get there, take the **7** train towards Manhattan and change in Jackson Heights to the **R** or **M** (towards Queens) and get off at Woodhaven Blvd.

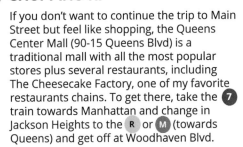

🍽 WHERE TO EAT

Flushing is an experience unlike anything you will see in NY! The iconic **Golden Shopping Mall** *(41-26 Main St)* was closed in 2019 for renovation, but you can check out the **New World Mall** *(136-20 Roosevelt Ave)*, with several restaurants, market, shops, lounge and even karaoke.

Joe's Shanghai - $$
13621 37th Avenue
Famous for its savory soup dumplings filled with hot broth & other traditional Shanghai dishes.

Shi Miai Dao - $ to $$
135-25 40th Road
Choose the side dishes and make your own noodles.

White Bear - $
135-02 Roosevelt Avenue (on Prince)
A region's icon specialized in traditional wontons. Like most restaurants there is no glamour, the big star is the food itself.

Sifu Chio - $$
40-09 Prince St
For a taste of Hong Kong Sifu Chio offers traditional noodle soups and dumplings.

Mapo BBQ - $$ - $$$
149-24 41st Avenue
Authentic Korean barbecue and they cook at your table.

Spring Shabu Shabu - $$
136-20 38th Avenue, 2nd Floor
Hot pot in a buffet style. You choose the ingredients and you can cook (boil) at your own table! Great value for money and several options for those who are vegetarian.

Spot Dessert Bar - $ to $$
39-16 Prince St
A bar specializing in creative desserts!

Ganesh Temple Canteen - $
143-09 Holly Avenue
In the Kissena Boulevard region, you'll find an Indian community with several dining options and the famous and oldest Hindu temple in the United States. The temple has a canteen that is open to the public and serves cheap and delicious traditional Indian food. The famous dosas are the house specialty.

Bodhi Village Inc
136-20 Booth Memorial Avenue
Vegetarian / vegan restaurant serving traditional Chinese dishes and sushi.

 Skyview Center | *40-24 College Point Blvd*

A mall with nice stores like Target, Marshalls and some outlet-style stores such as Converse, Forever 21 and Nike. Check out all the stores you can find on Skyview on the official website: *shopskyviewcenter.com*

 Jmart and New World Mall | *136-20 Roosevelt Ave*

It's a market (inside the New World Mall) and where you can find a little bit of everything: spices, meats, fruit, vegetables, frozen food, etc. The mall has some nice stores as well.

 Daiso | *40-24 College Point Blvd*

A $1.99 Japanese store chain which is famous for selling assorted products such as stationery, candy, decor, household items, etc ... The store is located at The Shops at Skyview Center.

 FEEL LIKE SHOPPING FOR BEAUTY PRODUCTS?

Check Club Clio, The Face Shop, Besfren Beauty, Nature Republic, MAC Cosmetics and even Macy's!

SUNDAY

> *I look out the window and I see the lights and the skyline and the people on the street rushing around looking for action, love, and the world's greatest chocolate chip cookie, and my heart does a little dance.*
>
> **Nora Ephron**

If you are traveling between May and October and you are doing today's itinerary on a weekend, I suggest starting the day on the first ferry to Governors Island (you might spend easily at least 2-3 hours there) and from there take the NYC Ferry to Red Hook (seasonal, check the website for schedule: *www.ferry.nyc*. Or you can simply assign a full day to Governors Island and one afternoon/evening for Red Hook if you have time. You can check tips on things to do in Governors Island on **page 60**.

If you wish to assign a whole day to Governors Island, I still recommend visiting Red Hook on weekends, when everything is open.

HOW TO GET THERE

 NYC ferry to **Red Hook**

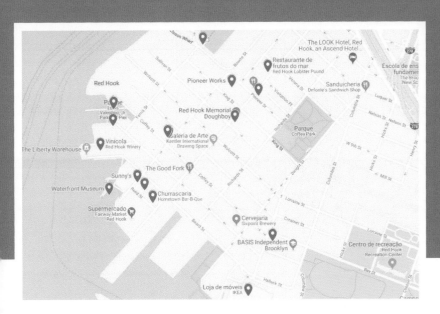

SUGGESTED BREAKFAST

- **Baked**
359 Van Brunt Street

RED HOOK

Red Hook was one of the first areas of Brooklyn to be colonized by the Dutch and it has a lot of history. Despite not being much explored by tourists yet, it is loved by the locals and there are many great experiences, I could not leave outside the guide.

HOW TO GET THERE

You can use the NYC Ferry by taking the South Brooklyn line in Manhattan or even other stops in Brooklyn and get off at the Red Hook stop. It costs $2.75 per ride and will give you nice views of Manhattan. Check the ferry times and stops on the app or website: *www.ferry.nyc/routes-and-schedules*

You can buy your ticket online, at the machines or when boarding. The boat usually leaves at the scheduled time. Don't be late!

LEAVING FROM MANHATTAN BY SUBWAY + BUS

Lines **2** **3** **4** **5** (**Borough Hall** stop) and **A** **C** **F** **R** (**Jay Street MetroTech** stop). From there you need to catch a bus, the B61. But check Google Maps for the best route.

1 The first stop of the day is the **Cacao Prieto** chocolate factory and the **Jane Widow** distillery, which are sister companies and share its space *(218 Conover St)* harmoniously.

■ The tours last around 1h, cost $15/person (2020) and are available on Saturdays and Sundays at noon, 2 pm, and 4 pm. If you want to do it at another time, you can book directly through the website, but the price is different.

- The tour goes through the factory so you can learn more about the history and process of cocoa - which comes from the Dominican Republic - until it becomes the final product. The tour is followed by an explanation about the production of drinks such as liqueurs and whiskeys and with a small tasting of both, included with your ticket.

TIP

Next, to the factory, you'll see the **Botanica Bar** *(www.cacaoprieto.com), a great alternative to enjoy drinks in a quieter environment.*

TIP

There is another nearby distillery, **Van Brunt Stillhouse** *(7 Sigourney Street |www.vanbruntstillhouse.com)* and they also offer tours and tasting. The tours take place on Saturdays from 2 pm -7 pm in the winter but check the website for an updated schedule in the warmer months. It costs $10 per person and you get the value back when you buy any bottle. Book your tour through the website.

2 From there you can take a brisk walk to **Louis Valentino, Jr. Park and Pier** *(Ferris St &, Coffey St Ferris St &, Coffey St)* for a gorgeous view of the Statue of Liberty.

3 If you want to taste authentic key lime pie, I highly suggest a quick stop at **Steve's Authentic Key Lime Pie** *(185 Van Dyke St - $).*

4 If you enjoy wine tasting, head to the **Red Hook Winery** *(175 Van Dyke St | www.redhookwinery.com/tastings)*, where you can have a wine tasting with 4 wines for $18. The grapes come from Long Island and other parts of New York State, but the wine is made right there. On Saturdays and Sundays at 1 pm, those who do the tasting are also able to join a free tour. It is usually 15 minutes long. If you want to do a private tour, taste wine straight from the keg and see how different wines are made, I recommend this one, but you need to book it in advance and it costs $35 per person.

5 From there, head to the **Waterfront Museum** *(290 Conover St)*, where you can learn a little more about the maritime history of Red Hook, inside an old boat, the most authentic experience possible! For schedules and information: *www.waterfrontmuseum.org*

FEELING HUNGRY? YOU HAVE SOME REALLY NICE OPTIONS IN THE AREA, BUT I'LL SUGGEST TWO:

🍽 WHERE TO EAT

Brooklyn Crab - $$
24 Reed St | www.brooklyncrab.com
Serving brunch on weekends and many dishes made with seafood. In the summer, it is a super busy and delightful place to enjoy the day.

Hometown Barbque - $$
454 Van Brunt St | hometownbarbque.com
For those who like meat, this is a good experience in a relaxed atmosphere with live music on Friday and Saturday nights.

6 I suggest a quick stop at Pioneer Works, a very interesting cultural space for art lovers (159 Pioneer St). The entrance price suggested is $10 but you pay what you want. When you enter, ask about the current exhibitions and decide if you really want to explore or not.

7 From there you can walk down **Van Brunt** to take the ferry or catch a bus to the subway station. If you have an appetite and feel like eating something else, the **Red Hook Lobster Pound** is right there at *284 Van Brunt St.*

💡 TIP

There is an **IKEA** *(1 Beard St)* store nearby! Once you are done you can board the "IKEA ferry" to Wall Street's Pier 11 in Manhattan. The ferry is free on weekends. On weekdays, It's only $5 per ride but free one-way with a $10 purchase at IKEA. There is a great view of the city. Check the schedule on the site: *www.nywatertaxi.com/cruise/ikea-express-ferry*

MONDAY

> *Every year the women of New York leave the past behind and look forward to the future. This is known as Fashion Week...*
>
> **Carrie Bradshaw**

From my perspective, Rockaway Beach is the best beach for swimming or even surfing in the NYC area. After the NYC ferry started running in the area, it got even more common for New Yorkers to spend summer days there.

 HOW TO GET THERE

Take the **NYC Ferry** at Wall Street/Pier 11 to Rockaway Beach, it costs $2.75 per ride. The ferry departs from downtown Manhattan, but if you're at Sunset Park in Brooklyn, it stops there as well. See the complete route here: *www.ferry.nyc/routes-and-schedules/route/rockaway/* The journey takes around 60 minutes and it is very nice. In the summer months expect lines especially on the way back so avoid weekends if possible. You can also take a bus in Rockaway to go to different spots.

Take the **train** (A) towards Rockaway (and/or switch to the (S) line at the Broad Channel station) and get off at the Rockaway Park Beach 116th Street stop.

There is no set itinerary for today, just enjoy the New York summer, walk along the boardwalk, taste the many food options and if you have kids with you, enjoy the playgrounds. Take cash, not all spots accept credit cards.

🍽 WHERE TO EAT

Tacoway Beach - $
302 Beach 87th Street
Tacos, guacamole, nachos, and drinks.

Rippers Burgers - $
8601 Shore Front Pkwy
Burgers, hotdogs, other snacks, and drinks.

Rockaway Brewing Company - $ to $$
415 Beach 72nd, Arverne
A craft brewery with several events. They serve some snacks too.

REGIONS'
MAP

Here you'll find each area's map! Just copy the link to your internet browser!

■ SUNDAY | DAY 01
bit.ly/Dia01Domingo

■ MONDAY | DAY 02
bit.ly/Dia02Segunda

■ TUESDAY | DAY 03
bit.ly/Dia03Terca

■ WEDNESDAY | DAY 04
bit.ly/Dia04Quarta

■ THURSDAY | DAY 05
bit.ly/Dia05Quinta

■ FRIDAY | DAY 06
bit.ly/Dia06Sexta

■ SATURDAY | DAY 07
bit.ly/Dia07Sabado

■ **SUNDAY | DAY 08**
bit.ly/Dia08Domingo

■ **MONDAY | DAY 09**
bit.ly/Dia09Segunda

■ **TUESDAY | DAY 10**
bit.ly/Dia10Terca

■ **WEDNESDAY | DAY 11**
bit.ly/Dia11Quarta

■ **THURSDAY | DAY 12**
bit.ly/Dia12Quinta

■ **FRIDAY | DAY 13**
bit.ly/Dia13Sexta

■ **SATURDAY | DAY 14**
bit.ly/Dia14Sabado

■ **SUNDAY | DAY 15**
bit.ly/Dia15Domingo

■ **MONDAY | DAY 16**
bit.ly/Dia16Segunda

COPYRIGHT

CREDITS

Content: Martha Sachser

Designer: Camila Aldrighi

Photography: Martha Sachser

Photo p.2 and 229: Alline Martim

Photo p.144: Tereza Sá

Special thanks to Anne Bongiovi

Printed in Great Britain
by Amazon

69483658R10126